T0293060

5-Star Career

5-Star Career

Define and Build Yours Using the Science of Quality Management

Penelope Przekop

Routledge
Taylor & Francis Group

A PRODUCTIVITY PRESS BOOK

First published 2022
by Routledge
600 Broken Sound Parkway #300, Boca Raton FL, 33487

and by Routledge
2 Park Square, Milton Park, Abingdon, Oxon, OX14 4RN

Routledge is an imprint of the Taylor & Francis Group, an informa business

ISBN: 9780367428082 (hbk)
ISBN: 9780367426354 (pbk)
ISBN: 9780367855260 (ebk)

DOI: 10.4324/9780367855260

Typeset in Minion
by Deanta Global Publishing Services, Chennai, India

Contents

About the Author

 **Penelope Przekop, MSQA, RQAP-GCP,** is a pharmaceutical quality and regulatory compliance industry expert, entrepreneur, artist, and writer. During her 30-year career, she has held leadership positions at Novartis, Covance, Wyeth, and Johnson & Johnson, and has worked with numerous Fortune 100 pharma companies. She is sought out for her broad and deep industry knowledge, regulatory expertise, and creative strategic approaches. She is the founder and CEO of PDC Pharma Strategy and also serves as the chief compliance officer for Engrail Therapeutics. She frequently writes, speaks, mentors, and delivers training on industry quality management and regulatory compliance topics.

She earned a BS degree in biology from Louisiana State University and an MS degree in quality systems engineering from Kennesaw State University. She is a graduate of the Smith College Program for Women's Leadership and the Rutgers University Senior Leadership Program for Professional Women. In 2018, Przekop and her older daughter founded Bra in a Box, which has been featured in *Real Simple* and *New York Magazine*. She is the author of *Six Sigma for Business Excellence* (McGraw-Hill) and four novels: *Please Love Me*, *Aberrations*, *Centerpieces*, and *Dust*.

She lives in the Greater Philadelphia Area with her husband of 30 years. Together they have two daughters and one grandson.

Introduction

Each man has his own vocation. The talent is the call. There is one direction in which all space is open to him. He has faculties silently inviting him thither to endless exertion. He is like a ship in a river; he runs against obstructions on every side but one; on that side all obstruction is taken away, and he sweeps serenely over a deepening channel into an infinite sea.

—Ralph Waldo Emerson

We live in a ratings-obsessed culture. Our shared preference for 5-star-rated products, books, movies, restaurants, etc., makes irrefutable common sense. At a time when information bombards us 24/7, logic, *that* common, is refreshing. We read online reviews and rely on ratings to make decisions about nearly every aspect of our lives. We compare cost with ratings and are thrilled to find a highly rated product or service at a price we can afford. However, the powerful quality rating system we've wholeheartedly embraced hasn't dovetailed with how we think and/or talk about the lives, relationships, or careers we want. *5-Star Career: Define and Build Yours Using the Science of Quality Management* tells you why it's time to do just that, why it also makes common sense, and exactly how to do it.

If you can relate to any of the scenarios below, I'm guessing you're not about to give your career, as it stands today, a 5-star rating:

- You're confused, conflicted, frustrated, or less than inspired about your career and/or where it's heading.
- You find yourself too often relaxing on a comfy couch Netflix binging with stray popcorn kernels in the folds of your favorite sweatpants when you should be job hunting or working from home.
- You often sit, zoned out, in your corner office-variety leather chair wearing a designer outfit, knowing how blessed you are to have such a fantastic job, yet also knowing it's not what you want to do.

- You're generally dissatisfied with your career; it's just not what you envisioned, it doesn't exist at all, or you feel like a fake who's going to get caught at any moment.
- You're confident that you're relatively smart and/or hardworking, but can't seem to get ahead, and you can't quite figure out why. Maybe you know why (or think you do) but don't have a clue how to make changes, or lack the confidence required.
- The people you work with are all *actual* jerks and/or you seem to morph into a jerk, for some odd reason, every time you walk into the office or open your laptop.
- At this point, you suspect that you should settle for a decent salary and benefits but sense that there should be more to gain from all the crap you have to do every single day.
- No matter how hard you work, those who can impact your career don't seem to appreciate it, or even fully understand what it is you're doing. Worse, maybe you understand the lack of appreciation because you yourself feel that what you're doing is ridiculous, boring, or glorified busy work.
- Weird career-related stuff you can't easily explain keeps happening. Whatever it is always ends up derailing your plan or otherwise holding you back. You feel like a magnet for bad luck.
- On top of it all, you're not sure what a 5-star career is for you; you're feeling listless and uninspired, yet you want *that* career. Perhaps once you have *it*, you'll know?
- You're feeling a little, or a lot, ticked off that everyone around you appears to be either thriving in a unique career that seemed to develop naturally over time, or they have the sort of job that has a clear progression based on years of experience. They all seem to have 4- or 5-star careers but not you.

The 5-star system you use not only to rate products and services, but to also make financial decisions evolved from the powerful science of quality management. This science, technology, engineering, and mathematics (STEM) discipline includes concepts and methodologies proven to result in customer satisfaction. The science gained major attention from Japanese political and manufacturing leaders determined to rebuild following World War II. They applied it to their manufacturing industry with intense commitment and ultimately emerged as a new global economic leader, revolutionizing the global economy by the 1980s. Less than a decade later, I entered the workforce.

As a young adult, I was convinced that focusing on my intellectual and professional growth was key to developing the type of self-identity I craved. Newly married, I had relocated from the Deep South to the East Coast, all the way to the suburbs of New York City. I was excited about reinventing myself. Like a flawed, fascinating character in a book or movie, I would put the past behind me and make a fresh start! I was determined to leave behind the oddly abusive childhood I'd shared with my brother. Just a year older, he was the only one who knew the story I left behind; in fact, he left it behind as well and moved to the West Coast, all the way north of Seattle. Well, the movies are right about one thing, eventually the past catches up with you. Mine began trying not long after I said, "Good riddance," and headed north.

That road I took led me straight into the pharmaceutical industry where I spent the next 30 years studying and implementing the science of quality management. As my career progressed and I fought the demons of my past, the science I was implementing at work began to influence my philosophies, shift my mindset, and provide a framework for my decisions. It became undeniably clear that the science used across the globe to build quality into products and services can be personally applied to build quality into a life and a career. *5-Star Career: Define and Build Yours Using the Science of Quality Management* not only tells you how to do that, it also includes my own story; the science of quality management turned out to be the missing link for me, and one that I'm passionate about sharing with you. This book offers the following benefits, which can have far-reaching, rippling impact for you. It will:

- Explain how the science of quality management can ensure customer satisfaction, which is what industry uses to gauge the quality of products and services.
- Relate that explanation to you on a personal level including how the basic concepts and components of the science apply to your career/job, and the path it has taken and can take.
- Challenge you to identify your authentic needs and desires following the thought process, research methodology, and data analysis

corporations rely on to understand their customers. I'll tell you how to do all of that, and provide a unique tool to help you gather and analyze the right type of data and information.

- Clarify the critical role that controlled systems and processes play in the science of quality management, the role they play in the personal application of quality management, and the surprising power they have to ensure intended outcomes.
- Explain how to apply the proven decision making methodology (used by industry) to identify the best possible process that leads to the career you deem as 5-star worthy, and to address the career elements that will satisfy your authentic needs and desire.
- Relay how risk-based decision making is not only key to identifying a process that ensures success, but also to addressing the unexpected curveballs that will surely come your way.

5-Star Career: Define and Create Yours Using the Science of Quality Management provides common sense, strategic context for personally implementing quality concepts that reflect your personal goals as well as your own definition of a 5-star life and career. You'll learn why the science of quality management has far-reaching applications and why *career* is a perfect place to start. The time is right to tap into the proven science behind the 5-star rating system. It makes sense, its effectiveness is irrefutable, and too many of us are tired of spinning our wheels. I don't know about you, but I don't have the time nor am I interested in spinning anything anymore. I'm ready to go big or go home, and hope you are, too.

Following is a brief, chapter-by-chapter peak at what you'll discover in the pages ahead:

Chapter 1: Give Me 5-Star Everything
The book begins with a reminder that the world isn't what it used to be and how that relates to quality. You'll learn that your life is *not* a process after all, nor is your career. You'll also find out why I rated my life as a *zero* at 19, and why.

Chapter 2: The Science of Quality Management
In Chapter 2, I'll introduce you to two brilliant nerds who took Japan by storm, how that eventually led to US legislation supporting the science of quality management, and why the entire world jumped on the quality bus.

Chapter 3: My Career Is a What?

Next, you'll read about blind spots and why they're so difficult to spot. I'll address how the mind can get set in stone as we grow up, and why mindset is so difficult to alter. You'll learn why systems and culture do not require permission to exist, and what this means for you. Lastly, you'll be challenged to accept that your career is a product that you can create.

Chapter 4: We're All Manufacturers

Chapter 4 will take you deeper into the idea that your career is a product that you can manufacture. I'll explain why manufacturers who create 5-star products know that taking the upfront time to follow the proven science is key to a quality outcome. You'll continue to follow my story and be challenged to consider how your personal story has impacted your philosophies and mindset.

Chapter 5: We're All Customers

If your career is a product, you're the customer of that product. In Chapter 5, I'll explain how being both the manufacturer and customer well positions you for success. We all start somewhere. I'll share more about where my life started and how it informed what I initially wanted, thought I wanted, and eventually *knew* that I wanted.

Chapter 6: Customers Have Problems

In movies, we watch problems from just about every lifestyle and scenario resolve within ~90 minutes. Bam! It feels good, or at least satisfying (especially, when it's a 5-star rated flick). You'll learn that, whether creating a 5-star widget or a 5-star career, time and patience are required. You'll meet the childhood demons my brother and I ran to opposite sides of the US to escape.

Chapter 7: We All Shop for the Big One

In Chapter 7, I'll focus on the disconnects between what we show the world and what we show ourselves, and between what we tell ourselves and what is true. I'll explain the one path we all consciously or subconsciously follow and why. I'll share how the science of quality management found me and how a surprising kink in my career showed me that running from the past is not the way to leave it behind.

Chapter 8: Manufacturers Build Trust

In this chapter, you'll learn why trust is also important in the personal application of quality management, and how you can begin to build trust in yourself. I'll explain how my brother's story eventually left me no choice but to accept the painful truth in our shared childhood. You'll begin to see why work/life balance is about much more than having time to do the laundry or tuck your kids in at night.

Chapter 9: Data Is King

Chapter 9 will prepare you to complete a personal story data-mining exercise that aligns with the quality management requirement of understanding customer drivers and needs. You'll learn quality management-based techniques for exploring your career history using a story data mining exploration tool that can be downloaded from www.penelopeprzekop.com (at no cost to you).

Chapter 10: Strategize for Quality

When you return to the book with the knowledge and insight gained from reading Chapters 1 through 9 and working through the story data mining exercise, I'll set the stage for the last quarter of the book and hit the go button. You'll be ready to personally apply the science of quality management to position yourself, set the strategy, identify a process, and make decisions about your career as it stands today, and where you plan to go.

Chapter 11: Claim Your System

In Chapter 11, you'll identify and establish your personal quality system, and understand what it means, the logic behind it, and why working within that system unleashes power you've always had, but may not have recognized, used, or understood.

Chapter 12: Define Your Process

This chapter will focus on risk-based decision making, including what that means, what it has to do with your personal data and information, and how powerfully it can influence the trajectory of your career. An out-of-control system cannot ensure a 5-star product. I'll explain why that is a proven reality, and why the sooner this is accepted, the faster you can manufacture the 5-star career you envision.

Chapter 13: Thinking Is an Ongoing Requirement

Moving forward with the topic of surprises, Chapter 13 will focus on how you can watch for curveballs, evaluate those that come your way, and make decisions considering the information and resources available within your personal quality system. I'll explain why it doesn't matter whose fault *it* is, and why understanding that in the context of quality management makes it a lot easier to accept. I'll end my own story and challenge you to begin a new one. Industries across the globe manufacture products and provide services that you deem 5-star worthy; they satisfy *you*. You can learn how to create a personal quality management-based framework, take specific steps to better understand your *authentic* self, and define what 5-star quality means to *you*. Then *you* can build it for *yourself* using the resources within *your* own system following the science of quality management. I'm passionate about sharing how this amazing science literally changed my life, and how it can also change yours.

1

Give Me 5-Star Everything

"Strive not to be a success but rather to be of value."

—Albert Einstein

Imagine it's 2020 again (just for a moment). You're finally in a clean set of PJs relaxing in your favorite comfy chair. It's been a long day of serial Zoom meetings in your makeshift office. Soft slippers are on and a blanket is in place. It's time for the guilty pleasure of online shopping. You're searching for the perfect surprise gift for dear Aunt Mabel. You recall the potato soup she always whipped up just for you. She dropped whatever she was doing to chat during your teen years, regardless of the topic. She's getting older now and seems lonely at times. You hope that a thoughtfully selected, unexpected gift will give her a little cheer tomorrow. You're determined to find a surprise that will have value and meaning to her (and that Amazon can deliver within 24 hours).

There it is! A kitchen widget made for her! She'll love its quirky edges and useful purpose, and it matches her pink polka dot kitchen. It's 3-star rated so you read several reviews to ensure that it won't fall apart upon arrival. Based on the cost, it seems fine. Aunt Mabel will give it 5 stars and that's all that matters. Sold!

You just experienced a successful shopping process guided by your plan, specifications, and goals, all with Aunt Mabel in mind. This new kitchen widget is valuable, and its value is the outcome of a successful process. It took longer than you imagined but you're thrilled. You know she's going to love it. Now you can get back to binge watching *Schitt's Creek*.

You could have saved yourself time by taking a different shopping approach. With one or two clicks, you could have transferred your

DOI: 10.4324/9780367855260-1

purchasing power to thousands of shoppers who know nothing about you or your Aunt Mabel. All you do is search for the highest-rated *Gift for Aunt* on Amazon and hit *Add to Cart*. Let's pretend you took that route. When the expensive, 5-star rated, newfangled, electric muffin stuffer arrives at Aunt Mabel's door, she opens it saying to herself, "What the heck? Well, that's sweet! It's the thought that counts." Then she shoves it in the back of the closet she spruced up last week with yellow-flowered wallpaper. She values that you thought of her; however, she doesn't value the muffin stuffer and wishes you hadn't spent so much.

Your shopping approach was more or less successful. You found an item and purchased it; you got the job done. If that's enough for you, all is well. However, if your goals were more aligned with the first approach, you may feel a disconnect, especially given that you spent more money than planned. Hey, maybe it wasn't your fault. You did your best, right? You had a busy day, and *Schitt's Creek* is so good! Netflix is addictive, and the world just isn't what it used to be. Later that night in bed, you clutch your body pillow thinking that Aunt Mabel probably won't know how to use that fancy kitchen appliance. She just needs to get out more. If she would just do that, you wouldn't have to worry about her so much. Your last thought as you drift off is, "Oh well, life's a process. And after all, a kazillion people gave it 5 stars."

We live in a world obsessed with ratings. We prefer to purchase 5-star products, read 5-star books, eat at 5-star restaurants, and watch 5-star movies. We love reading online reviews and heavily rely on ratings to make decisions about nearly every aspect of our lives. We compare cost with ratings and are thrilled when we find a highly rated product or service at a price we can afford. Quality ratings are a fantastic way to evaluate and select actions to take and decisions to make. Let's face it: we even rate and categorize our experiences with those around us using our own internal criteria. This doesn't make us judgmental; it makes us human. First impressions represent a cornucopia of ratings, all subconsciously tabulated within seconds. According to research at New York University led by Daniela Schiller, there are regions of the brain that sort information based on its personal and subjective importance and summarize it into an ultimate rating, a first impression. Meeting people activates the same region of the brain responsible for assigning prices to objects. Vivian Zayas, a professor of psychology at Cornell University, and her colleagues, found that people continue to be influenced by another person's appearance even after interacting with them face-to-face. In a university study, first impressions formed simply from looking at a photograph predicted how people felt and thought about the person after a live interaction that took place one to six months later.

THE WORLD ISN'T WHAT IT USED TO BE

The incredible technological advances of the last 25 years paved the way for Fortune 500 companies to bring a quality rating strategy directly to their customers. Technology and the science of quality management met, and the 5-star quality rating system was born. Consumers ate it up; it makes logical sense and appeals to the senses. Now nearly every company in every industry on the planet is on board. And we love it!

Most likely, you would not love to publicly rate the quality of your life, or the lives of those around you, including careers, on a 5-star quality scale. Many companies require managers to assess and discuss employee ratings with more senior management on an annual basis. I've never met a manager who enjoys that process or who would want to make the information publicly available. It's safe to say that no one wants to write an online review of a neighbor's, sister's, or co-worker's life or career and assign a quality rating. Yet many of us *internally* compare our lives, job performance, and careers to those around us. The mysterious *they* say that you should refrain from doing so and they're correct. But it's tough not to do it! It's hard to see other people succeeding in areas where you're coasting through or even floundering. It's painful to feel lonely when all your friends are married with kids, which is the life you wanted to have by now. It's frustrating when you can only buy a used car when your neighbors or relatives are driving new ones. Telling your kid that they can't go on the school band Disney trip this year, even though all their friends are going, feels awful. Or how about telling your kid that you're having cereal for dinner again because money is tight? On the flip side, maybe you feel like a selfish jerk because you dread going to work every morning, despite having a salary that would cover a year's worth of 6-course meals for 20? Every life and career is different. I believe that whether in specific moments, or over long stretches of time, both your life and career can be pretty darn close to perfect on a deeply personal level. You will always be challenged to accept and deal with the full range of emotions that make you human, and for that reason, there will always be dips, loops, and calls for unexpected change. In many cases, those are the times that offer opportunities to choose continuous improvement over continuous *movement*, which is what will bring you closer to long-term perfection.

How would you rate your career, as it stands today? Would you give it a one? Is it a three? What are your standards? If you rate your career as a five without too much thought, this book may not be for you. I'm truly happy for you! However, you may want to stay tuned to ensure that your rating is properly defined. If you think your career is a five but don't *feel* like it is, keep reading so that you can find out how to understand this disconnect. On the flip side, if you think your life is a one but aren't too concerned about it ... that's a disconnect of a different kind. I'm betting that most people land in the 3-star zone, at the crowded top of the bell curve. Who wants to spend their life there? Do you shop for 3-star rated widgets? Are you excited about watching the latest 3-star rated movie this weekend? Why not? Well, because the widget you need, and the movie are products. You're the customer. In that role, you prefer a particular level of quality given the cost incurred. There's nothing more valuable than the time you have between the day you're born and the day you "take the train," as my Dad likes to say. Every single day of your life, you pay a fee from that time bank. It's tough to fully grasp or even focus on this when you're young; that's natural. Nobody wants to be a morbid 22-year-old. Even at my age, it is not a thrilling topic. Yet, it is a hard truth that I consider the universal motivator.

YOUR LIFE IS NOT A PROCESS

I don't want to spend even one unit of the most valuable currency I have on mediocrity, or worse, absolutely nothing. I'm writing this book because I'm passionate about sharing a new, yet proven, approach that can infuse your career with the 5-star quality you want or crave. You're wired in a beautiful, authentic way yet you're tasked to live in a world that continually challenges, shifts, questions, and wounds based on a need for common ground. You're biologically driven to be true to yourself yet compelled by various tugs and twists to satisfy a multitude of individuals who move in and out of your life. You've likely been encouraged not to care what people think, to be yourself, yet you're constantly thrown into situations where others seem to have incredible influence over key aspects of your life and career. You struggle to understand what they want, expect, and deserve from you, even if at a subconscious level. And you weigh all that against your own desires, struggling to make the best choice, or to do the right thing, time after time. It can be exhausting. Sure, some of us feel this more than others, or realize that we feel this. In the end, regardless of how humans first stood on two feet, complex and fascinating biological processes keep you ticking at the center of modern-day constructs. When things get confusing or go wrong, many people coach themselves, thinking, "Oh well, life's a process." There's one problem here; your life is not a process, nor is your career. A transaction is occurring. The life and the career you have at any given moment are products that incur a cost. Don't waste the valuable time you're spending every day; you can't cancel the subscription.

If you want 5-star everything, you damn sure should get a 5-star quality life and career. The life you have, right now, is the result of a process just like the gift Aunt Mabel ended up with resulted from a shopping process. Your career requires a huge chunk of your valuable daily time payment. You may have heard about work-life balance. You may have also heard that your boss and company CEO are not likely to attend your funeral. (They might, depending on the scenario, but you get the point.) Theoretically, it's not a great idea to sacrifice what's truly important in life for what is *just* a job or a career, and especially not for one that *just* pays the bills, or worse, one you dread showing up for every day. Yet, the work you do eight or more hours a day has a significant impact on your quality of life. How you spend your time and energy, your physical location, who's standing next to you, what challenges you, gives you joy, a headache, or a sense of accomplishment *is* your life. It doesn't matter if it happens during eight hours on the job, five hours on the beach, or three hours in the yard with your kids. Your career is a critical component of how you perceive and define the life you have and how you feel about it. It's not easy to consider your career as merely an add-on to all the other things that define your life. There's nothing wrong with expecting high quality in return for the precious hours you give to your career. Despite what your gut may be telling you (in more ways than one), a high salary does not guarantee career satisfaction. Quality is not defined by monetary value.

If you're wondering what *can* guarantee satisfaction, you're reading the right book. Applying the science of quality management to your personal development will result in 5-star quality. This has been proven repeatedly in multiple industries across the globe for the last 120-plus years. In every example, success hinges on obtaining an accurate understanding of how the primary customer defines quality. Cue the 5-star rating system. The logic behind it is compelling and makes common sense. In fact, you might be surprised to know that there is an entire science behind it, one large and complex enough to move a nation from desolation to economic power following World War II, provide enough content for numerous PhD programs by the year 2000, and more recently, impact global commerce in lightning speed.

Fortune 500 corporations like Nike, Walmart, Berkshire Hathaway, Johnson & Johnson, Apple, and GE aim to create 5-star rated products and services that delight customers. I've spent 30 years working with Fortune 500 companies to implement, evaluate, and improve quality management systems whose purpose is to ensure product quality and customer satisfaction. As I navigated through the challenges, hiccups, successes, and failures that came my way, a connection between the science of quality management and my life took shape. I began to internalize the concepts I was executing in my day-to-day work and found what proved to be the missing link for me, and possibly for you. Applying the science of quality management on a personal level differs from the longstanding, inspirational approaches that urge you to think positive, make good decisions, get an education, work hard, delay gratification, etc. In recent years, many phenomenal authors, psychologists, and educators have provided new insight on how to improve your life and career, including:

- Kelly McGonigal has helped increase our understanding of stress and willpower and how they can both be harnessed for amazing results in her books *The Upside of Stress: Why Stress is Good for You and How to Get Good at It*, and *The Willpower Instinct: How Self Control Works, Why It Matters, and What You Can Do to Get More of It*.
- Carol Dweck taught us about the extraordinary power of mindset in her book *Mindset: The New Psychology of Success*.
- Malcolm Gladwell brilliantly showed us how a combination of seemingly insignificant elements can build magic in his book, *The Tipping Point: How Little Things Can Make a Big Difference*.

These experts and others provide fantastic, logical advice that isn't always easy to implement long term. Dr. Phil, Oprah, and other dynamic motivators continue to provide powerful fuel for success, which is wonderful, for those who have the right engine. You can think positive, get an education, keep yourself informed, strive to make good decisions, and work smart and hard, yet still find yourself in a career that doesn't feel worth all the time you've spent, whether it's only been a year or 30 years.

During my long struggle to overcome a troubling childhood and become the best version of myself, all while building a technical career, I began incorporating quality management concepts into my personal thought process at home and at work. I found out that the science proven to result in 5-star rated products and services can also result in a 5-star rated life. You may be thinking, "Wait, this book is about my career not my life." True, but we've established that a large chuck of your banked time is spent on the work that you do. It's all intertwined. It's nearly impossible to look at your career in a vacuum. This book focuses on career rather than the whole shebang. However, if you believe that who you are before and after work doesn't influence your career, that's the first thing you need to unlearn to accept the power you have to successfully manage the quality of your career. Armed with a solid understanding of the basic concepts and commitment to their application, you can build and/or improve any aspect of your life.

MY ZERO LIFE

My life did not begin with a 5-star quality rating by anyone's standards, certainly not by my own, which is what truly matters. My brother and I were raised in the Deep South by a mentally ill mother who was emotionally and physically abusive despite her good intentions. It was painful. By 17, I knew that I was exhibiting some self-destructive behaviors but had no idea what it meant or how to change. Even when I knew intellectually that a choice was poor, I felt emotionally driven to make it. I sensed that I was too smart to be so stupid. I also thought that a smart girl would understand what was happening in her life. That kind of girl, the type I wanted to be, would know what to say and do, and why, especially when it came to relationships. A smart girl would know *when* to say and do all the things that needed to be said and done. I don't recall thinking about whether life was a process or a product; nobody I knew talked about such things. I felt an overwhelming lack of control and direction that was suffocating. I'd felt that way for a long time, and I wasn't sure why. I graduated from high school early and went to college.

At 19, I rated my life as a huge ugly 0, and attempted suicide. That night I sat in my childhood bedroom wearing a colorful Madonna-inspired outfit that worked well with my big, teased hair, Bible in hand. I had a sensation of sitting in a vacuum that I would never escape. I begged God to somehow let me know that my life had value. I told Him that I would open the Bible and point to a verse. It would be His message to me, a technique often used in our Deep South Bible Belt Sunday School classes. I closed my eyes and pointed. I can't remember exactly what the message was on that night 30-plus years ago, but it was something like Proverbs 6:12–14:

> Let me describe for you a worthless and wicked man; first, he is a constant liar; he signals his true intentions to his friends with eyes and feet and fingers. Next, his heart is full of rebellion.

I thought surely this is a mistake! God would want me to live! Is He saying that I'm a rebellious liar? Jesus loves me, this I know, right? I decided to try again. I pointed to a scripture, and then another, and another and another, desperate for a reason to believe that I should stick around. Every verse was similar. I was devastated and lonely in a way that I still find difficult to describe. Convinced that even God couldn't seem to locate my intrinsic quality, I went forward with my plan to swallow all of my troubled mother's psychiatric medication.

As I swallowed those pills, I couldn't have imagined, in my wildest dreams, that I would have the life and career I have today. I felt like a failure at 19, and I even failed at suicide. After spending several days in the hospital, including a two-day stint in the intensive care unit, I emerged patched up with nowhere near the level of healing I needed to improve the quality of my life. I faced a long, lonely journey and decided that I would fall back to my childhood mantra: alone at least I have myself. I would never give up again, not like that. Somehow, I would build the kind of life I wanted, although I still had no clue how to do it. This was not some kind of exuberant, renewed feeling of sudden inspiration; it was a terrible, foreboding feeling. It was exhausting. It was a realization that I couldn't even leave my life behind, so I just had to keep trying. Mixed in there, however, was the faint recognition that I was glad that I was still alive although I couldn't think of any reason to celebrate.

Today I'm a corporate quality management expert who has worked with Fortune 100, 500, and smaller niche pharmaceutical companies including Johnson & Johnson (J&J), Pfizer, Merck, Lilly, Novartis, Glaxo Smith Kline, Amgen, Vertex, Alexion, Covance, Daiichi, and Otsuka to improve product quality and customer satisfaction. I have a bachelor's degree in biology and a master's in quality systems engineering, and 30-plus years of industry experience. I'm the author of five books, including four novels and *Six Sigma for Business Excellence* (McGraw-Hill), an internationally published and translated business book that teaches managers at all levels how to apply proven quality management concepts to their day-to-day work using common sense strategies. I've also written for various magazines and online publications. I've been a columnist for *Pharmaceutical Manufacturing Magazine*, and I'm a frequent speaker on quality management concepts. My fiction and narrative nonfiction writing have been praised by *The New York Times* bestselling authors and publishing industry professionals whom I admire. My figurative expressionist artwork has been represented and shown in galleries in New York City, Philadelphia, San Francisco, and other key markets throughout the US as well as globally. It's also included in the permanent collections of two Italian museums.

How did I go from rating my own life a zero to having my own unique 5-star career? As you can imagine, it's complicated, as most lives are. The truth is that no one has it easy. Life is tough. I don't know the details of your life, how you got where you are today, or where you hope to be next year, or in 20 years, but I do understand the boredom, disappointment, curiosity, despair, failure, drive, heartache, and/or hope that possibly prompted you to pick up this book. You have a unique history and mindset, in addition to many other factors, that contributed to where you find yourself today. I won't pretend that it's simple. Through my ups, downs, backward and forward steps, I stumbled across a unique solution. Sharing it with you means a lot to me from both an intellectual and emotional perspective.

As my life and career evolved, I embraced and applied the fundamental quality management concepts listed below in a deeply personal way:

1. Life is not a process nor is your career. Your career is a *product* created by your process.
2. Quality is defined by the customer; the quality of your product (career/life) is defined by you.
3. Quality cannot be accurately rated or improved until it's defined.
4. You are 100% responsible for your product.

One or more of the concepts above may initially seem counterintuitive, which is one of the reasons I'm writing this book. They may also remind you of the Pygmalion effect, which is all about how grand expectations can lead to remarkable results, and low expectations can lead to poor results. When applied to yourself, this is often referred to as self-fulfilling prophecy. It also sounds a bit like the power of positive thinking. I believe in all of that; however, none of it is quality management. Hello! It's time to open your mind. I'm coming in to explain this proven science, how it led me straight to where I sit today, and its potential to change the trajectory of your career.

KEY POINTS

1. First impressions represent a cornucopia of ratings, all subconsciously tabulated within seconds. We rate and categorize our experiences with those around us using our own internal criteria. This doesn't make us judgmental; it makes us human.
2. You will always be challenged to accept and deal with the full range of emotions that make you human, and for that reason, there will always be dips, loops, and calls for unexpected change. In many cases, those are the times that offer opportunities to choose continuous

improvement over continuous movement, which is what will bring you closer to long-term perfection.

3. You're wired in a beautiful, authentic way yet you're tasked to live in a world that continually challenges, shifts, questions, and wounds based on a need for common ground.

4. You're biologically driven to be true to yourself yet feel compelled by various tugs and twists to satisfy a multitude of individuals who move in and out of your life.

5. Life is not a process. The life you have, right now, is the result of a process.

6. The life and the career you have at any given moment are products that incur a cost. Don't waste the valuable time you're spending every day; you can't cancel the subscription.

7. When talking about how the science of quality management can be applied to your career it's nearly impossible to look at that career in a vacuum. If you believe that what goes on outside your work doesn't influence your career, that's the first thing you need to unlearn to accept the power you have to successfully manage the quality of your career.

8. If you're looking for an overnight, easy solution, it doesn't exist.

BIBLIOGRAPHY

Carol Dweck. *Mindset: The New Psychology of Success* (Ballantine Books, 2007).

Daniela Schiller, Jonathan B. Freeman, Jason P. Mitchell, et al. A Neural Mechanism of First Impressions. *Nature Neuroscience* 12, 508–514 (2009).

Kelly McGonigal. *The Upside of Stress: Why Stress is Good for You and How to Get Good at It* (Avery, 2016).

Kelly McGonigal. *The Willpower Instinct: How Self Control Works, Why It Matters, and What You Can Do to Get More of It* (Avery, 2013).

Malcolm Gladwell. *The Tipping Point: How Little Things Can Make a Big Difference* (Bay Back Books, 2002).

Penelope Przekop. *Six Sigma for Business Management: A Manager's Guide to Supervising Six Sigma Projects and Teams* (McGraw-Hill, 2005).

Vivian Zayas, Gul Gunaydin, and Emre Selcuk. Impressions Based on a Portrait Predict, 1-Month Later, Impressions Following a Live Interaction. *Social Psychological and Personality Science* 8, 36–44 (2017).

2

The Science of Quality Management

"Quality is never an accident; it is always the result of high intention, sincere effort, intelligent direction, and skillful execution; it represents the wise choice of many alternatives."

—William A. Foster

When the science of quality management met online shopping, a global economic and cultural phenomenon was born: the 5-star rating system. The *baby* grew like a weed and moved into the mainstream like a rocket. Now the kid is everywhere, inconspicuously infusing the science of quality management into our modern culture. In this book, I'll share how the obscure science behind how you shop may be your missing link. The proven science used by companies across the globe to create 5-star products can also be used to create your 5-star career.

You didn't sign up for a history lesson and this is not a textbook. However, to appreciate how the science of quality management can be applied to your life and career, you'll need a basic understanding of how global manufacturers and service providers rely on it to ensure quality and customer satisfaction. The figure below provides a visual representation of how the science of quality management has evolved (Figure 2.1). What took root in dark, dusty factories during the late 1800s and the early 20th century developed through modern-day manufacturing, made its way into global regulated industries and corporate initiatives, and dove straight into the mainstream online shopping experience.

Quality is essentially the grade of excellence. The term first surfaced between A.D. 1250 and 1300. It's human nature to desire products and services that deliver the value we expect. We select products and services

DOI: 10.4324/9780367855260-2

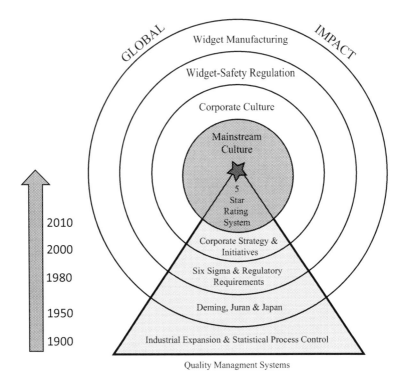

FIGURE 2.1
The evolving science of quality management.

that can solve a problem, whether it's a prom dress, a vacation package, or a new set of cookware. We make the purchase with the expectation that our problem is going away. In the end, the level of quality we assign to that product or service hinges on our satisfaction. This is nothing new, just like most basic aspects of being human. That's why the existence of an entire science around it may be a bit surprising. In a world where no two individuals are alike, imagine the complexity introduced when manufacturers or service providers are tasked with figuring out who their key customers are and what they want. The goal is to understand what problem the customers need to resolve as well as what solutions they may have already tried and why they didn't work. The simple idea of giving someone what they want becomes quite tricky.

Back in the Middle Ages (500–1500 A.D.), final products were often inspected essentially to make sure that they weren't lemons. This wasn't a particularly scientific approach, yet it helped to tease out obvious errors.

This approach went on for centuries. It wasn't until the early to mid-20th century that the science of quality management began to emerge. The focus was still on the final product but the application of statistical theories to control quality gained interest. The concept of establishing set standards and guidelines was developed, along with the idea of testing products, processes, and services against documented requirements. This seemed to work OK in smaller operations; however, as global industry expanded, larger volumes of products were manufactured in one day, staff numbers increased, and difficulties surfaced. Early leaders in the field began to gain a voice in US manufacturing. Staff checked specific product components along the production line, rather than relying on inspection of only the final product. This updated the focus to preventing problems earlier in the production line. The idea was to catch an error earlier so that it could be corrected before it resulted in a defective product. This saved time and money. Instead of tossing out a fully created bum product, corrections could be made earlier, resulting in fewer defective products at the end.

Whether you're 22 or 52, you can avoid having a bum career by making corrections as early as possible. To do that, you'll need a process to identify and/or to avoid missteps in the here and now. Think of all the time, energy, and even money (your cost) that can be saved. Think of the heartache and disappointment that could already have been avoided. Well, it's not too late. Stay tuned.

JAPAN EMBRACES TWO BRILLIANT NERDS

No, this is not about Steve Jobs and Bill Gates; it's about W. Edwards Deming and Joseph Juran. Getting back to our history lesson, after World War II, it was the Japanese who took the science of quality management to heart. The products that emerged as they rebuilt didn't have the best reputation; although cheap, they were not in demand due to their inferior quality. At a time when the top Western quality management experts were struggling to gain widespread acceptance, a few brilliant Japanese leaders plucked them out from under the noses of the US business community. W. Edwards Deming (1900–1993), one of the foremost US experts in quality management, was invited to speak to the Japan Medical Association in 1950. Through a series of seminars, Deming taught the basics of statistical quality control plainly and in detail to executives, managers, engineers, and researchers of Japanese industries. Then, in 1952, the Japanese Union of Scientists and Engineers (JUSE) invited over another early champion of quality management, Joseph Juran (1904–2008). When he finally got there in 1954, he was met by top Japanese company executives. Soon after, he began teaching courses on managing quality to top and middle management, an approach that had generated pushback in the US. In contrast, Japan passionately embraced the science illuminated by Deming and Juran. By the 1970s, the high quality of products made in Japan began to transform the global economy. The small country had evolved from total disaster to becoming the global economic leader, throwing the US into crisis mode by the early 1980s. There was no denying the powerful impact that the science of quality management had on product quality, customer satisfaction, and the bottom line.

Deming's 14 Points for Management, first presented in his classic 1982 book, *Out of the Crisis*, condensed his theory and provided a roadmap for leaders who wanted to transform their organizations. The manufacturing world was ready to listen. Deming's 14 points for management apply to organizations of all sizes and in all industries, both manufacturing and non-manufacturing. His 14 points can also be applied personally to life and career. Deming's theory is based on understanding the difference between common and special cause variation. Deming knew that, unless a change is made to the manufacturing system, the system's capability will remain the same. This holds true for your career. You must change your system to change your capability.

Deming told us that a system's capability is determined by common variation, which is inherent in any system. Just as our weight is not the same each day, there are small inherent systemic changes that take place within systems. You can't control a common cause of variation. Neither companies nor individuals should hold themselves accountable for these events. Common variation in business and personal systems can be caused by factors such as downturns in the economy, weather events, and even COVID-19. On the other hand, special cause variation is situational and can be avoided. Examples of special cause variation include operator error, faulty equipment setup, or incoming defective raw material. If you're interested in learning more, I encourage you to explore all of this on your favorite search engine.

On August 10, 1984, the movie, *Revenge of the Nerds*, was released. The movie tagline is: "They've been laughed at, picked on, and put down. But now it's time for the odd to get even! Their time has come!" It's about a group of bullied college outcasts and misfits who resolve to fight back for their own peace and self-respect. (If you're too young to know about this movie, check it out.) As a college sophomore, trying to understand myself, this seemingly silly movie resonated with me. It also hit a mainstream cultural nerve. Bill Gates and Steve Jobs, both born in 1955, had come out of their garages in the late 1970s; the microcomputer revolution was underway. Deming and Juran finally had the respect they deserved. The world was on the brink of phenomenal change.

THE US GOVERNMENT CREATES AN ACT

In response to the global economic situation, the US government passed the Malcolm Baldrige National Quality Improvement Act in 1987. The Act recognized that the leadership of the US in product and process quality had been challenged strongly (and sometimes successfully) by foreign competition and the growth in productivity of the US had improved less than that of our competitors over the previous two decades. The findings also noted that American business and industry were beginning to understand that having products or services of mediocre quality costs companies as much as 20% of sales revenues nationally and that improved quality of goods and services goes hand in hand with improved productivity, lower costs, and increased profitability. They knew that strategic planning for quality and quality improvement programs, through a commitment to excellence in manufacturing and services, was becoming essential to the well-being of our economy and our ability to compete effectively in the global marketplace. It supported the growing belief that improved management understanding of the factory floor, worker involvement in quality, and greater emphasis on statistical process control can lead to dramatic improvements in the cost and quality of manufactured products.

By establishing the Malcolm Baldrige National Quality Award to recognize US organizations for their achievements in quality and performance and to raise awareness about the importance of quality and performance excellence as a competitive edge, the Act challenged companies to improve quality. The Malcolm Baldrige National Quality Award program includes Criteria for Performance Excellence, which focuses on a systems perspective. The program defines systems perspective as managing all the parts of your organization as a unified whole to achieve your mission, ensuring that the individual parts of your organization's management system work together in a fully interconnected, unified, and mutually beneficial manner. Applying a systems perspective to your life would mean managing all the parts as a unified whole to achieve your mission. It also means ensuring that all the various parts of your life work together in a fully interconnected, unified, and mutually beneficial manner. Compartmentalization is out, just as silos are frowned upon in corporations. You may have heard about breaking down organizational silos. Now it's time to break down the silos within yourself.

For over 25 years, the Baldrige Criteria have been used by thousands of US organizations to stay abreast of ever-increasing competition and to improve performance. For today's business environment, the criteria have been updated to help organizations respond to current challenges: openness and transparency in governance and ethics; the need to create value for customers and the business; and the challenges of rapid innovation and capitalizing on knowledge assets. Whether a business is small or large, is involved in services or manufacturing, or has one office or multiple sites across the globe, the criteria provide a valuable framework that can help plan in an uncertain environment. The criteria are designed to help organizations use an integrated approach to organizational performance management that results in the delivery of ever-improving value to customers, contributing to marketplace success, improvement of overall organizational effectiveness and capabilities, and improvement of organizational and personal learning.

Read that last sentence a couple of times. Using an integrated approach to self-management that results in delivery of ever-improving career value for the cost incurred, while also contributing to your success and improving your overall effectiveness, capabilities, and learning, may be exactly what you need. This stuff makes sense, and it's exactly what I needed. The Baldrige Criteria are built on the following set of interrelated core values and concepts:

- Systems Perspective
- Visionary Leadership
- Customer-Focused Excellence

- Valuing People
- Organizational Learning and Agility
- Focus on Success
- Managing for Innovation
- Management by Fact
- Societal Contributions
- Ethics and Transparency
- Delivering Value and Results

These beliefs and behaviors are embedded in high-performing organizations as well as in high-performing individuals. Later, we'll focus on how these core values and concepts apply on a personal level.

THE ENTIRE WORLD JUMPS ON THE BUS

By the mid-1990s, governments and industries across the globe had realized that they would need to jump on the bus or get the hell off the road. The following information is only a fragment of the story. If you're interested in knowing more, I encourage you to Google on, my friend. On the other hand, if you're struggling not to fall asleep, it's safe to skip ahead to Chapter 3. You can always come back to check relevant facts or to gain additional knowledge that supports the meat of the book. If you do skip ahead, I urge you to read the Key Points found at the end of this chapter before diving into Chapter 3.

The International Organization for Standardization

In 1987, The International Organization for Standardization (ISO) published ISO 9000, which has evolved into a family of standards that assist organizations of all types and sizes to implement and operate effective quality management systems. Its history can be traced back some twenty years before that, to the publication of government procurement standards. The key principles of ISO 9000 series are customer focus, leadership, engagement of people, process approach, improvement, evidence-based decision making, and relationship management.

The ISO 9000 series has been adopted globally and at least one million organizations have been ISO certified. The standards have shifted over the years but generally remain true to the principles described above.

Six Sigma and Regulated Industries

By the mid to late 1990s, global regulatory health authorities, such as the US Federal Drug Administration (FDA), had developed regulations and guidelines based on the science of quality management, influenced by Deming and the ISO. In the pharmaceutical industry, the regulatory focus on quality management began in manufacturing. Those responsible for developing and enforcing regulations in industries such as aerospace, nuclear, and pharmaceutical were early adopters of the concepts due to their laser focus on safety. In the meantime, another methodology, called Six Sigma, had evolved and reached the pharmaceutical industry. It was supported by Deming's theory of management, particularly the emphasis on common and special cause variation, which is a key focus of Six Sigma methodology when determining how to improve processes. Six Sigma is a disciplined, data-driven approach and methodology for eliminating defects (driving toward six standard deviations between the mean and the nearest specification limit) in any process – from manufacturing to transactional and from product to service. Six Sigma at many organizations simply means a measure of quality that strives for near-perfection. It can be called "Six Sigma," or it may have a generic or customized name for the organization like "Operational Excellence," "Zero Defects," or "Customer Perfection."

Math Warning! Six Sigma got its name from a statistical concept, but the approach goes well beyond data and figures. With that said, we can't move forward without understanding just what Six Sigma is and what it says about processes. In statistics, the lowercase Greek letter sigma "σ" is the symbol for standard deviation, which describes the degree of variation in a dataset, a group of items, or a process. A Six Sigma level of quality means that there are fewer than 3.4 defects, or deviations from the standard, per million units produced (Table 2.1). It's a technical measure of customer satisfaction. A unit can be any product or service. The principles of Six Sigma can be applied to many different situations. For example, if, in a sample of 100 widgets, 5 defects were found, that would mean 0.05 or 5% defective widgets, or that 95% of the widgets were acceptable. According

TABLE 2.1

Relationship between Sigma Level and
Defect Frequencies

Sigma Level (Process Capability)	Defects per Million Opportunities
2	308,538
3	66,807
4	6,210
5	233
6	3.4

to the sigma conversion table (Table 2.1), this percentage of acceptable units falls between sigma levels 3 and 4. At a three-sigma level, you can expect 66,807 defects per 1 million widgets, and at a four-sigma level you can expect 6,210 defects per 1 million widgets.

A major management philosophy developed around the six-sigma measurement described above. It focuses on customer satisfaction, data-driven management, and process improvement. As you read earlier, the customer defines quality. Customer satisfaction is the key determinant of quality. If a product satisfies the customer or meets the customer's specifications, then it's acceptable; otherwise, it is defective in some way. To define the quality of any product, one must fully understand customer needs and specifications. Accurate identification of customer requirements is at the heart of the Six Sigma philosophy. To calculate a sigma level that realistically reflects customer satisfaction, you must understand what your customer wants. For example, a widget that is perfect in your eyes may not be perfect in the eyes of your customer. So, Six Sigma not only provides management tools to figure all this out, it also prescribes a step-by-step methodology for their application. DMAIC (an acronym for Define, Measure, Analyze, Improve and Control) (pronounced dM-MAY-ick) refers to a data-driven improvement cycle used for improving, optimizing and stabilizing business processes and designs.. The DMAIC improvement cycle is the core tool used to drive Six Sigma projects, and it can also be used to improve your life and career.

Although ISO 9000, the Baldrige Criteria, and Six Sigma are each unique, the underlying concepts of all three center around process focus, customer focus, collaboration, data-driven management, and strategic planning for quality. Table 2.2 assigns the key concepts of these three

TABLE 2.2

Comparison of Key Quality Management Concepts with Criteria of Three Quality Management Systems

Key Concepts	ISO 9000	Baldrige Criteria	Six Sigma
Process focus	Process approach and continual improvement	Process management	Process management and improvement focus
Customer focus	Mutually beneficial supplier relationships	Customer and market focus	Genuine focus on the customer
Collaboration	Involvement of people	Human resources focus	Boundaryless collaboration
Data-driven management	Factual approach to decision making	Measurement, analysis, and knowledge management; business results	Data- and fact-driven management
Strategic planning for quality	Leadership and systematic approach to management	Strategic planning and leadership	Proactive management, drive for perfection, and focus on achieving zero defects rather than a zero employee error rate

quality management concepts to these five critical concepts. As you look (if you're still here and awake), consider how these concepts could potentially be applied to how you manage all the parts of your life, including your career.

All the content in this chapter relates to you and your career. The intent is to give you a basic understanding of how the science of quality management is used in industry and how the underlying concepts and philosophies drive success. No matter who you are or what type of job you have or may be looking for, your skill or educational level, I'm betting that, like me, your goal is to end up with products and services that will not fall apart or disappoint in any way. Whenever that goal is not achieved, you feel cheated; your time and money have been wasted. It's not a great feeling. You're a dissatisfied customer. It's also not a great feeling to spend time on a career that falls apart or disappoints you in any way. The exciting news is that you're not only the customer who wants a

5-star career; you're also the one and only person who has the power to create (or manufacture) it. Once you understand the relationship between *you* as the customer and *you* as the manufacturer, nothing can stop you in your quest for quality.

KEY POINTS

1. To appreciate how the science of quality management can be applied to your life and career, you'll need a basic understanding of how global manufacturers and service providers rely on it to ensure quality and customer satisfaction. (If you're not sure you've got it, I encourage you to read this chapter again. Grab a cup of coffee, if needed.)

2. Whether you're 22 or 52, you can avoid having a bum career by making corrections as early as possible. To do that, you'll need a process to identify and/or to avoid missteps in the here and now.

3. Just as our weight is not the same each day, there are small inherent systemic changes that take place within systems. You can't control a common cause of variation. Neither companies nor individuals should hold themselves accountable for such events.

4. Using an integrated approach to self-management, that results in the delivery of ever-improving career value for the cost incurred, while also contributing to your success and improving your overall effectiveness, capabilities, and learning may be exactly what you need.

5. Using what is referred to as the DMAIC cycle, Six Sigma ties the approach together into a neat package that can be applied across many functions and industries, and to your life and career.

6. Applying a systems perspective to your life would mean managing all the parts as a unified whole to achieve your mission. It also means ensuring that all the various parts of your life work together in a fully interconnected, unified, and mutually beneficial manner. Compartmentalization is out, just as silos are frowned on in corporations. You may have heard about breaking down organizational silos. Now, it's time to break down the silos within yourself.

7. Although the quality programs, philosophies, awards, etc. mentioned in this chapter are each unique, they share the underlying concepts of process focus, customer focus, collaboration, data-driven management, and strategic planning for quality.

8. The exciting news is that you're not only the customer who wants a 5-star career; you're also the one and only person who has the power to manufacture it. Once you understand the relationship between *you* as the customer and *you* as the manufacturer, nothing can stop you in your quest for quality.

BIBLIOGRAPHY

W. Edwards Deming. *Out of the Crisis, reissue* (The MIT Press, 2018).

3

My Career Is a What?

"A good system shortens the road to a goal."

—Orison Swett Marden

The first of four fundamentals (introduced in Chapter 1) that skyrocketed my ability to build a 5-star career bridges the gap between the industrial and personal application of the science of quality management.

1. **Life is not a process nor is your career. Your career is a *product* created by your process.**
2. Quality is defined by the customer; the quality of your product (career/life) is defined by you.
3. Quality cannot be accurately rated or improved until it's defined.
4. You are 100% responsible for your product.

Accepting that your life, and your career, are products is the key to understanding how the science of quality management applies to a career. First, let's consider why life isn't a process. How many times have you heard or said that life is a process, that it's filled with twists and turns you don't always understand? You try to do the best you can, yet you remain at the mercy of a secret, undefined process called LIFE. And life happens at work, too. After all, everything happens for a reason, right? If you're a fierce believer that life is a process, you're confident that you'll figure it out eventually; you'll learn from it and do better next time, and perhaps it's all happening for some pre-ordained reason that you remain positive about and trust. This positive belief system certainly is admirable. It makes you feel better and enables you to cut yourself a break. But how

DOI: 10.4324/9780367855260-3

long is the whole thing going to take? In this scenario, you assume that the confusing process of life will eventually result in a deep, abiding feeling of satisfaction across the board, including in your career. When that feeling doesn't come soon enough, or only in one or two areas while the rest of your life is floundering, you're disappointed and confused. It gets harder and harder to build yourself back up, even when you value resilience. It's easy at the beginning. It gets harder as you grow older and use up year after year of your banked time. You may begin to wonder what it's all for after all. You might eventually settle on, "Well, the bills are getting paid. I'll do all the things I've been dreaming of when I retire."

Some people believe that life is a process due to religious upbringing and/or beliefs. If you were raised like me, you were taught that you're simply not going to understand God's plan; you shouldn't question God or His methods. Stop trying, they told us. My brother and I were taught to simply trust in Him, which often left me feeling like I had little to no control over my life, which I suspect was not what He intended. They told me to let go of my control; give it all to God. I tried and that didn't work so well, although I don't blame God. If your belief that life is a process isn't religiously driven, it may be the Universe you believe in. The Universe knows! There's absolutely nothing wrong with faith, hope, and all of that; in fact, it's extremely important. However, out of context, it can create a mindset that holds you back rather than actively moving you forward. You wait and wait and trust and trust, squelching your questions about why things aren't going your way, often feeling guilty for even having them. I've been there, done that. If you believe in God, then you probably believe that He doesn't make mistakes. Ergo, you are not a mistake. You don't have kinks, defects, or bad programming. This means that God has already given you everything you need to be the best possible version of yourself.

If it's not God or the Universe that has you believing that life is a process, you may simply be one of the billions out there operating with an inaccurate definition of the term *process*. If so, let's clear that up immediately. According to dictionary.com, the primary definition of *process* is a systematic series of actions directed to some end: to devise a process for homogenizing milk, or a continuous action, operation, or series of changes taking place in a definite manner: the process of decay. Businessdictionary. com defines *process* as a series of logically related activities or tasks (such as planning, production, or sales) performed together to produce a defined set of results. The keywords and phrases in these definitions are *logically related, systematic,* and *a definitive manner.* Life in all its complexity is rarely logically related, systematic, and/or rarely takes place in a definitive manner. If you believe that it is logical, systematic, or definitive, or attempt to make it so, you will fail. Systematic and definitive processes include specific elements that are known, controlled, and monitored to produce a specific outcome. We absolutely cannot control every aspect of life or every possible scenario that can and does occur, which are numbered in the billions; therefore, we cannot expect, hope, or dream this thing called *life* into being a process.

Life is also not God's nor the Universe's process. Since you have free will, and no two individuals are genetically alike, neither God nor the Universe can control billions of unknowns either! Okay, sure, perhaps God can, but does He? If so, why would He give you free will? I'm thinking that He trusted His creation enough to give you a bit of rope; perhaps so that He can focus on the bigger picture. No wonder so many people feel like giving up. No wonder people feel confused, helpless, and out of control. No wonder people believe they should just settle for the life and career they have rather than expecting more. I've been there and it makes me sad.

Your life, as it stands today, is a product and so is your career. There's a proven science that tells us a product is produced within a system, and that the system can be controlled to ensure the pre-specified quality of that product. It tells us systems do not require permission to exist, and therefore, any product you hold in your hands resulted from a system. The science has evolved and is staring you in the face every time you shop online. A 1-star rated product was produced in a system and a 5-star rated product was produced in a system. It's time to harness that science in new ways, one of which is to produce a 5-star rated career.

Understanding more about systems is our first stop. Industries across the globe rely on quality management systems (QMS) designed to ensure product quality and customer satisfaction. The QMS ensures that the product or service is produced as planned. A QMS includes documentation, quality checks, statistical methods to evaluate data obtained throughout the product planning and production process, and methods to ensure early identification and corrections of errors. Electronic systems can be used in powerful ways to support a QMS, but a QMS is much more than an electronic system. In fact, a QMS can exist without that aspect. By definition, a *business system* is the organization (a structure, responsibilities, procedures, and resources) needed to conduct a major function within a business or to support a common business need. Systems are usually made up of multiple processes that take an input, add value to it, and produce an output. You operate within a system when cooking a meal. To put it simply, through the execution of several processes that involve shopping, chopping, mixing, peeling, etc., you take ingredients (inputs), add value to them (frying, mixing together, etc.), and produce dinner.

There are a lot of people who don't particularly like the idea of systems. Maybe that describes you or perhaps you know someone who wants to "rail against the system" and hopes to "stick it to the man." What they don't realize is that systems exist whether they want them to or not. Systems are not inherently bad. We should all rail against poor systems. One way we can do that is to learn more about them, why they exist, how they can be managed to ensure positive outputs, and how they can be improved. The power of harnessing and using systems properly has been widely accepted in manufacturing for decades, with nonmanufacturing businesses such as hotels, banks, and insurance companies picking up speed behind them. It may behoove individuals to gain clarity on this topic. In many cases, it may be a case of trying to stick it to something that, if managed properly, is the answer.

BLIND SPOTS ARE DIFFICULT TO SPOT

When developing a good strategy for managing a particular system, the first step is often philosophical. A *philosophy* is a set of principles for guidance in practical affairs; essentially, it's the beliefs or opinions that guide your thoughts about all kinds of practical, daily life scenarios. For example, one might say:

> In the practical affair of raising children, my philosophy is that kids should listen to their parents, all children deserve to have a good education, parents should not put labels on their kids, and adults should ensure the safety of children.

It's helpful to understand how a philosophy and mindset differ from and dovetail within a system. A good example is an educational system. The system is built on the philosophy that all children deserve a good education, that governments are largely responsible for providing education to children, and that education should be, for the most part, consistent for all children. Believing all that doesn't make it happen. If one has a mindset (outlook or attitude) required to move this philosophy from conceptual to concrete, they must create a system in which that can happen. The system may consist of teachers, buildings, methods of testing, finances, a leader, kids, teaching materials, etc. And each of those parts of the system will need processes that work well and dovetail within that system to get things ticking like clockwork.

Your philosophy is essentially the overarching belief system that guides your thought process, whether consciously or subconsciously. Belief systems can be built on numerous things, ranging from fact to outright fiction, from reality to illogical ideas that may just work in the end. Whatever it is, it's yours, although it may or may not be accurate, a great one, or like your neighbor's. Philosophy shapes *mindset*, which is an attitude, disposition, or mood. In her book *Mindset: The New Psychology of Success*, Carol Dweck educates readers about the power of basic beliefs, how they "affect what we want and whether we succeed in getting it." Dweck focuses on two mindset types: fixed and growth, and how the two impact our lives. When you drill down, the mindset of an individual is surely nuanced, regardless of whether it falls to the side of fixed or growth.

Mindset is like a tight weave fused by concrete. Once a conclusion is stuck in there, it's not easy to remove or shift. A conclusion trapped in a concrete weave somewhere in your brain can create a blind spot. These spots can subconsciously steer you in one direction despite your preference, or deep need, to head the other way. It can be quite discouraging. Blind spots can convince you that all your disappointments are due to your own faulty wiring. They can also convince you that it's all someone else's fault. Either way, you're the victim of your own story. Some people consciously have these thoughts and even verbalize them. For others, they're subconscious beliefs that ooze out in job interviews, staff meetings, conversations, emails, etc. Blind spots can ultimately create a vibe around you (*which we will talk about soon*). This is a critical and challenging issue to resolve.

People are driven by their mindset; they view the world from their own perspective, regardless of how true, accurate, or realistic it may be. It's one of those human nature things. Once set, it's tough to change. I became tangled up in my own flawed mindset for years. It was a mix of: (1) my authentic personality and disposition (aka, DNA), (2) the disconnect between what I was taught and what I was shown, (3) my role in a dysfunctional family trapped in a never-ending tornado caused by a mentally ill mother, (4) societal norms where I grew up, at the time I grew up (1970s and 1980s Deep South), (5) the books I read, and (6) much more, I'm sure. Breaking free required many stops and starts, false starts, setbacks, and start overs, all while continuing to interact with the mother who essentially added extra concrete to the weave.

When a blind spot finally clears, paving the way for shifts in mindset, it strikes you as incredible, almost crazy, that you didn't see it before. I'm still in that mode. I'm not sure that I'll ever move out of it. As wonderful as it is to have clarity, I want to reach back to my younger self, through the years and past all the pain I put myself through. I want to go back and somehow shorten the winding road she's starting down. I would go to the night she sat pointing at her Bible and tell her how much intrinsic value she had, just waiting to be unleashed. (I would also suggest that she do her part in shortening the big hair fashion fad as quickly as possible.)

THE BIRTH OF MINDSET

By the time I was 12, I'd spent years watching, even studying my mom's inconsistent and illogical behaviors. In fact, I'd become an expert at explaining a great deal of it away, either to myself, or to others. In my mind, she was a delicate, special creature who needed someone like me around. People were constantly misunderstanding her; they didn't know her like I did. They lacked insight. I was 12 and that was my mindset the day she announced that something quite miraculous was going to happen, and that it was important that I be prepared. We were in my parents' 1970s station wagon, the kind that had a rear-facing third seat in the far back and paneling on the exterior sides. I still remember what street we were on when the words came out of her mouth. I remember the exact businesses we drove past as my mind took in her important message. It's a frozen moment in my mind. To outsiders, we likely appeared to be a typical mother and daughter, running errands on a Saturday, mom dressed impeccably, me in hand-me-downs, tall for my age with braces. Mom had taken me to yet another deliverance session, which was not quite your average Saturday afternoon errand. During these anointed, life-changing, fantastical appointments, my mother ministered to others, delivering them from Satanic demons in the name of Jesus. I was usually told to stay in another room, or wait outside, while she changed lives on God's behalf. That was more important than me, and it was assumed that I knew that. I did know that. My mother and God were spectacular. I was just there. That day we had gone to the home of a local, well-known, faith healer. She and my mother were ministering together; it must have been a challenging case. The healer's 19-year-old son took me to his room and taught me how to play backgammon. He was handsome and kind. Neither of us discussed what was going on in the other room. On our way home in the station wagon, mom told me the important news: God had informed her that my Daddy was going to die so that she could marry the pastor of our church, the same man who had delivered her from evil a few years back. Through him, God drove an entire army of demons from my mother. Then he ushered her into what she believed was her true calling, demonic exorcism, which became her favorite topic. She told me many years later that after her deliverance, she stopped hearing all the terrifying voices that had been telling her to kill herself.

SYSTEMS AND CULTURE DO NOT REQUIRE PERMISSION TO EXIST

Like individuals, companies develop a philosophy and mindset, and together they create the company culture. Once engrained, company culture is also difficult to shift; it can become set in concrete. It can cause blind spots that derail entire organizations. Most people can easily find a few words to describe their company or workplace culture. Like systems, culture develops, whether you want it to or not. It's not waiting for anyone's permission to exist or to get started. Leaders of award-winning companies who understand the science of quality management know this and accept their responsibility to shape and support a company culture that inspires all employees to aim for the highest levels of quality. The philosophy and mindset that stick start at the top and provide a framework that can powerfully steer the evolution of company culture.

Your personal philosophy and mindset also develop a culture around you; think of it as a vibe. You may be thinking that this sounds something like that secret shared in Rhonda Byrne's bestselling book, *The Secret*. I agree that thinking positive brings positivity to your life. Byrne calls this positive manifestation. Be positive and all will get better. Sounds easy, right? Well, remaining positive 24/7 for an entire lifetime is difficult, and I'm not sure it's healthy. It's tough to keep all that going in the middle of things like the year 2020, which covers a ton of examples. I don't know about you, but people who are constantly, extraordinarily positive cause me to pause and wonder if they're for real. Sometimes I can't help but question the authenticity involved in 24/7, lifelong positivity. Although I believe in the Secret and admire those who practice it, I wonder how long they can keep smiling. I find myself imagining what might happen when all those positive vibes get a bit too heavy to hold. I know what that feels like. No matter how big the smile, there comes a time when you just can't muster up that twinkle in your eye for one more second.

Can you clearly describe your personal philosophy and/or mindset? If so, can you provide evidence that it's helping you be the best possible version of yourself? If you can't clearly describe your philosophy and/or mindset, join the crowd. These are often tough concepts to define on a personal level. Your foundational philosophy and mindset were formed by the dovetailing of a million experiences occurring at various moments in your physical, intellectual, and emotional evolution.

In recent years, neuroimaging studies have demonstrated that the adolescent brain continues to mature well into the 20s. Most of the input that shaped your initial core philosophy and mindset was tucked away as your developing brain received, processed, and reacted to it, deciding which existing path it should take, or what new pathway it should build. The scientific evidence on how memory works further supports that it's not always easy to fully understand why you think the way you do; you're often influenced by details of your life that you can't even recall. Each thought you have is essentially the result of the years-long biological process your brain went through to end up what it is today. Instantaneous reactions to everything you see, hear, or touch are the result of complex, behind the scenes, mental processing. In something faster than a nanosecond, it's like your brain goes through one of those gigantic math equations professors work on in movies (think *Good Will Hunting*). That is exactly why making a permanent change to these two aspects (philosophy and mindset) of who you are requires serious commitment. My aim is that once you understand and accept how powerful philosophy and mindset are, and the pivotal role they play in the outcome of every moment of your every day, you'll be excited about making that commitment.

COMMIT OUT LOUD

Corporations typically have a shared mission and inspiring vision, but they also need consistent guiding principles or policies. Policies are among the highest-level elements a leader can use to create the shared company philosophy and mindset needed to spark, grow, and embed a focus, respect, and pride for quality into the culture. A quality policy is a general statement of a company's commitment to quality; however, its function and purpose are critical components to success. A quality policy establishes the philosophy and mindset of the organization and lays down roots that the entire quality management system needs to thrive. The policy is a brief statement that aligns the purpose and strategic direction of the company and lays the framework for all future quality objectives. It states the company's commitment to meeting customer requirements, as well as any regulatory requirements that apply. I'm sure you won't be surprised to hear that quality policies can be empty words on paper. If the senior leaders of a company fail to embrace, respect, and honor those words, they mean nothing. Actions ultimately speak louder than words; however, formally documenting a commitment has significant impact. In the science of quality management, the quality policy is the marriage license that officially declares to the world:

> This company is committed to quality. We will incorporate that commitment into all that we plan, do, and produce; it will weave through every process we develop, decision we make, and action we take from this day forward. As a company, we acknowledge that this may not always be the easiest thing to do, but it is always the right thing to do.

Making a commitment in your personal life may seem like a big ask at this point. You may not be fully convinced or may have a red flag popping up in your head for one reason or another. This is exactly why the science of quality management has never seemed too exciting outside of the product manufacturing floor, that is until every marketing department in every corner of the world realized the power of the 5-star rating system. So, hold on to your hat, hang in there, and keep reading. Be aware that deciding to commit doesn't trap you in lifelong servitude to quality management concepts. Just as in marriage, there are ways to leave it behind. However, my hope is that you'll fall in love with the idea of spending the time needed to explore how a new mindset and philosophy based on quality management may be your missing link, just as it turned out to be mine.

It's never too late; I don't care who you are. Philosophies, mindsets, and systems can be shifted. They can change. I hope your road hasn't been too challenging. If it has, take heart! I've come to acknowledge that there are some wounds and regrets that time cannot fully erase; however, time provides opportunities for healing and renewal, a shift in composition, and a scar capable of fading. I love tattoos that incorporate scars or physical deformities, transforming them into magnificent, creative images. That's the idea! That's exactly what you can do with your history, no matter what it includes, how bad it is, or what you missed. Creating those miraculous tattoos requires the artist to gain a comprehensive understanding of what they are tasked to transform. To create beauty, they must explore the damage. They study it until they see the beauty that they can use their skills to unleash. Recovery from childhood emotional abuse doesn't happen overnight, and sometimes outcomes are uncertain. Real change of

When Corporate Leaders Embrace Quality Management
5-Star Products Become a Reality

PHILOSOPHY
We are personally dedicated to quality. We respect the science of quality management. It leads to 5-star products.

MINDSET
Our combined corporate attitude, disposition or mood (culture), influenced by our core philosophy, creates an organizational mindset critical to success.

SYSTEM
We work within an established quality system that includes a set of correlated parts required to create 5-star products.

PROCESSES
We document efficient processes that ensure consistent delivery of 5-star products to our customers. We respect our processes and understand their value.

5-STAR PRODUCTS
We monitor internal deliverables throughout our processes to ensure quality and to support continuously improvement of both our process and our products.

Employees enjoy being at work.

Quality Culture

FIGURE 3.1
When corporate leaders embrace quality management: 5-star products become a reality.

any kind doesn't happen with a snap of the fingers. It may have taken many years, but I defined the life I wanted. I connected the final dots and put all the diverse pieces of my personal life and career together to establish a much more productive and efficient approach for developing not only the 5-star career I wanted, but also a 5-star life. Figure 3.1 shows how *philosophy, mindset,* and *system* work together to support the development of 5-star products or services. These three elements can also work together to support the development of your 5-star career.

KEY POINTS

1. Accepting that your life, and your career, are products is the key to understanding how the science of quality management applies to a career. There's a proven science that tells us a product is produced within a system, and that the system can be controlled to ensure the pre-specified quality of that product.
2. Life in all its complexity is rarely logically related, systematic, and/ or rarely takes place in a definitive manner. If you believe that it is logical, systematic, or definitive, or attempt to make it so, you will fail.
3. Industries across the globe rely on QMS designed to ensure product quality and customer satisfaction. The QMS ensures that the product or service is produced as planned. Systems are usually made up of multiple processes that take an input, add value to it, and produce an output. You operate within a system when cooking a meal.
4. A philosophy is a set of principles for guidance in practical affairs; essentially, it's the beliefs or opinions that guide your thoughts about all kinds of practical, daily life scenarios. Your personal philosophy and mindset also develop a culture around you; think of it as a vibe. Your foundational philosophy and mindset were formed by the dovetailing of a million experiences occurring at various moments in your physical, intellectual, and emotional evolution.
5. Mindset is like a tight weave fused by concrete. Once a conclusion is stuck in there, it's not easy to remove or shift. A conclusion trapped in a concrete weave somewhere in your brain can create a blind spot.

6. Each thought you have is essentially the result of the years-long biological process your brain went through to end up what it is today. Instantaneous reactions to everything you see, hear, or touch are the result of complex, behind the scenes, mental processing.
7. It's never too late; I don't care who you are. Philosophies, mindsets, and systems can be shifted. They can change and work together to support the development of the 5-star career you seek.

4

We're All Manufacturers

"If you can't describe what you are doing as a process, you don't know what you're doing."

—W. Edwards Deming

If you embrace the concept that the career you want is a product, and that you are the manufacturer of that product, the possibilities become endless. In his bestselling book, *Flow: The Psychology of Optimal Experience*, Mihaly Csikszentmihalyi wrote that the control of consciousness determines the quality of life. This applies to the quality of your career, too. Just as industry purposefully and systematically develops a product, you can consciously control, and therefore purposefully and systematically develop a career. Figure 4.1 depicts the widely accepted high-level purposeful and systematic process for product development based on the science of quality management.

On the contrary, rather than following the product development process shown in Figure 4.1, imagine that a company decides that they don't have time for all those extra steps and are not convinced of their importance. Instead, they set out to develop a product by applying the three-step, loosey-goosey process shown in Table 4.1. They can call it a process; it is going to be their process. However, it lacks both purpose and a systems approach, among other things.

If the loosey-goosey company is lucky enough to eventually produce a fantastic product, they will likely have wasted many years and lots of money. This business approach is risky, inefficient, and frankly, not too smart. It doesn't work well for product manufacturing nor is it ideal for *career* manufacturing. Unfortunately, this is one of the many loosey-goosey

DOI: 10.4324/9780367855260-4

PRODUCT DEVELOPMENT PROCESS

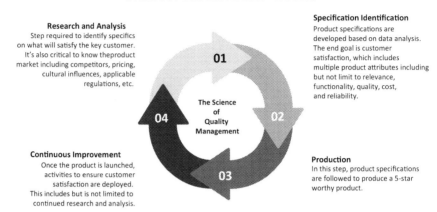

Research and Analysis
Step required to identify specifics on what will satisfy the key customer. It's also critical to know theproduct market including competitors, pricing, cultural influences, applicable regulations, etc.

Specification Identification
Product specifications are developed based on data analysis. The end goal is customer satisfaction, which includes multiple product attributes including but not limit to relevance, functionality, quality, cost, and reliability.

Continuous Improvement
Once the product is launched, activities to ensure customer satisfaction are deployed. This includes but is not limited to continued research and analysis.

Production
In this step, product specifications are followed to produce a 5-star worthy product.

The Science of Quality Management

01 02 03 04

FIGURE 4.1
Product development process.

processes that well-meaning individuals follow hoping to build what they envision to be a 5-star career. In that scenario, it often looks something like the process shown in Table 4.2.

When applied to your career, the loosey-goosey process above may seem quite intuitive. It may sound like what your parents, high school guidance counselor, a teacher, or perhaps your grandfather told you. However, it's not a purposeful, systematic process intended to produce a specific outcome/product. Many people make what seem to be well-thought-out, immediate career decisions with the assumption that making the right choice at that time will naturally lead to the next step, another weighty decision to make when the time comes. Unfortunately, next steps are often

TABLE 4.1

The Loosey-Goosey Company Manufacturing Process

The Loosey-Goosey Company Manufacturing Process Our Motto: Don't Stop Believing!	
Step 1	We will start by focusing on making the absolute best first required decision. It's all about taking the best possible first step! That will lead us forward!
Step 2	We will focus on the work required to execute our selected first step. Each person will give it their all!
Step 3	We will hyper-focus on that step, while keeping our eyes and ears open for what to do next. We don't know what that is, so we'll wait for the universe to reveal it to us. Everyone will continue to do their best, stay alert, and it will pay off!

TABLE 4.2

The Loosey-Goosey Career Manufacturing Process

My Loosey-Goosey Career Manufacturing Process My Motto: I Believe!	
Step 1	I will begin by focusing on making the absolute best first required decision, whether that is selecting a trade program, a college, or my first job. It's all about taking the best possible first step. That will lead me in the right direction!
Step 2	I will focus on putting in the work required for what I've selected as my first step. I will give it my all!
Step 3	I will remain hyper-focused on that step, while keeping my eyes and ears open for what to do next. I'm not sure what that is, but if I do my best and watch for opportunities, they will come.

slow to come, or a decision that seemed right at the time was made in a vacuum or was supported by inaccurate assumptions. You can't predict the future. However, you can define a desired outcome and then apply the science of quality management to ensure that outcome. That's what the best manufacturers in the world do on an ongoing basis. Without this approach, all those carefully considered decisions may lead nowhere other than where you'll be working for the immediate future.

WHO HAS TIME FOR THIS?

In Chapter 3, your *career* as it stands today, or on any given day, was defined as a product that results from a process. Products are manufactured. Who manufactured your career as it stands today? What's that? I can't make out what you're saying. Some of the responses I *have* heard over the years are listed below. (I've even heard similar words coming out of my own mouth.)

- I'm stuck here because of that nasty boss I had for years. He held me back!
- I am where I am today because of my dysfunctional family. If I had grown up in a better environment, I would be farther along by now.
- It's my mom's fault. She's wonderful but her tears dissuaded me from joining the military. My dream was to have a military career; she took that from me, and I was never able to find another passion.

- My wife convinced me to forego the one job that would have changed everything for me. She didn't want to move too far from her family. After that, I never caught another big break.
- Having three kids slowed down my career. I wouldn't trade having my kids for anything; they are my pride and joy. It's just that they're adults now, and I'm stuck.

If you commit to manufacturing a 5-star career, you must view yourself as the manufacturer who is 100% responsible for the quality of your career. Imagine that you were 100% responsible and had the power to manufacture your career as it stands today, take a few minutes (or hours) to consider the following questions about your approach to date:

Planning

1. Was there an initial high-level plan for your career?
2. Was a process established prior to production of the career?
3. Did you assess the resources required for production and identify any existing gaps?
4. If there were gaps, did you assess the level of risk they introduced to the process?
5. Did you develop a plan to resolve any gaps that held significant, unacceptable risk to the development of your product?

Execution

1. Did you follow an established process?
2. Did you determine what might be acceptable variations beyond your control versus those that you could control?
3. If something truly beyond your control happened (like COVID-19), did you assess the level of risk that was introduced?
4. If something unfortunate happened (you got a new boss who acts like a jerk and your work life became a living hell), did you determine the root cause and subsequent corrective or preventative actions? Did you purposely minimize the damage or redirect?

If you're thinking that carving out the time to do all the above in a purposeful and systematic way seems a bit like overkill or busy work, join the crowd. You've just experienced the thought process of nonmanufacturing operational staff across the globe who still believe that what they're doing on any given day (for instance, finishing a report by end of business today) is more important than taking the up-front time required to establish, support, and follow a quality management system. Remember this, the science emerged from manufacturing; there continue to be some late adopters in nonmanufacturing and service industries and functions. Yes, I realize that you never thought or said that quality isn't important; you only said that the stuff listed above seems like overkill. All those nonmanufacturing folks adjusting to the importance of quality management never say that quality lacks importance either. In fact, if you ask nonmanufacturing operational professionals in the pharma industry if quality is important, I guarantee that the vast majority will state that quality, defined by patient safety and data integrity, always comes first. If that's true, then why do some continue to push activities proven to assure quality to the bottom of their budgets, strategic plans, and to-do lists? There's a long and a short answer to that. The short one is that it's a relatively new science they don't yet understand. What they are doing is akin to you declaring that quality is your top priority while choosing to disregard the proven science of quality management. Good luck all around. I prefer not to rely on luck. Why would I accept such an unnecessary risk?

The science of quality management has proven repeatedly over the last 100 years that believing in and valuing quality does not make quality happen. Quality must be designed into the system (remember systems are there whether we realize it or not) that generates the product, and then purposefully managed. Ignoring this fact, being too busy to do it, or pushing the associated actions to the bottom of the priority list incurs a cost down the road. In a world where instant gratification is king, focusing on what's down the road can be challenging. This is yet another reason why industry leaders commit out loud to quality, and why company-wide commitment to quality is about much more than doing an excellent job in the moment or double checking for typos.

I THOUGHT I HAD A GOOD PROCESS

My dad was a high school teacher, guidance counselor, and vice-principal responsible for academics. He influenced me to value education above almost everything else in my life. This was particularly important to me and my future given all the inconsistencies I faced growing up. Having a mentally unstable mother made each day feel uncertain and scary. My dad's focus on reading and education appealed to my intellectual side in a way that helped my world feel a bit steadier. It gave me a clear destination, solid land ahead that I could focus on and move toward. Without the concrete belief that education could somehow set me free, I'm not sure what would have happened to me. It was a fantastic focus for me. By the time I was in high school and even college, I knew in my gut that if I got one or more degrees, I'd be okay. I'd get a decent job. Then I'd do an excellent job at my job. Then I'd get a better job. I would be secure. I'd be independent. I'd have my own life and no matter what, I'd be able to take care of myself. It seemed so simple. I trusted that the world knew what I knew, and that it would all work out. The unsteady life I'd known would become calm and consistent. And with that calm, somehow, I'd be happier. I'd know what choices to make and why. I'd finally be able to stand on solid ground.

Surprise! While all the above is true in many ways, having a degree doesn't make emotional issues go away, the world isn't always consistent, and building a career isn't quite that simple. I was not prepared for office politics, salary negotiations, difficult supervisors, long commutes, the exhaustion toddlers bring, adjusting to married life, processing a difficult childhood, public speaking, multitasking, being someone's boss, teamwork, and all the other combined realities of adulting and working. The factors at play differ depending on your personal story, responsibilities, industry, and your physical work environment. Earning a diploma, certification, or degree and developing a skillset does not independently guarantee anything. They are a beginning. Everything, anything, or absolutely nothing can potentially happen as you spend the precious time you have to be alive. The exciting news is that you are a manufacturer, and with that comes tremendous power. As the manufacturer of your career and your life, you can create the outcomes you want.

As noted in Chapter 1, numerous books filled with expert advice are available to us. They always seem to make sense. They're inspirational. During college, not long after my suicide attempt, I began reading those types of books. *Your Erroneous Zones* by Wayne W. Dyer and *How to Win Friends and Influence People* by Dale Carnegie particularly resonated with me. They were filled with new thought-provoking ideas that prepped me for a shift in mindset. Yet it wasn't enough. It was as if they were speaking directly to me, saying, "Here's the model. Here's what you can be, Penelope.

People who do this are happy and successful. Now believe in yourself and get started." While I embraced the message, I couldn't figure out how to execute what I was reading in a way that made sense for me. Then I felt frustrated, believing that I should be smart enough to figure it out. I had no idea how to get started, or keep it going, given the specifics of my own story. To simply *start* felt disingenuous, as if I were skipping critical steps that I couldn't ignore or define.

Here's a list of some of the common career advice we read in these types of books:

- Have the right mindset.
- Get and stay organized.
- Believe in yourself.
- Manage your time.
- Focus on the goal.
- Just do it.
- Get an education.
- Stick to one thing.
- Don't sell yourself short.
- Be confident.
- Ask for the promotion.
- Manage difficult people well.
- Improve your public speaking skills.

You may have read many of these terrific books, too. You may have gotten organized, spoken up, and trained yourself to focus on the positives, yet you're still not where you want to be. After studying and implementing the science of quality management for years, I realized that although the advice above represents no-nonsense, direct concepts and provides vision, it is a bit shortsighted. In the context of quality management, these power-packed statements are akin to saying: "Build a product people love and they will buy it." Unfortunately, it's not that simple.

WHEN, WHERE, AND HOW DID IT GO WRONG?

That's a loaded question, and you're the only person on earth who can figure it out. I have no idea when, where, or how anything went wrong for you, but I do know that you can figure it out, and then use that knowledge to finally manufacture a 5-star career. Let's start by considering a typical scenario. What is presented here as *typical* may not fit your situation exactly; it's intended to provoke thought about how you arrived where you are at this moment. (But I do believe the scenario is quite common.) (Figure 4.2.)

If you happened to follow this typical scenario and you're completely satisfied, congratulations. It is possible. (However, because you're reading my book, I'm guessing that you may not be.) The typical scenario below wasn't your fault, either. The world is not a fair place. I didn't choose to be created by a mentally ill mother; it wasn't fair that I had to deal with that when the other kids in the neighborhood did not. Children starving around the world aren't choosing to be hungry. It's horrible and it's not fair, but it is happening. I hate that! I also know that waiting to hand your power to a person, group, cause, boss, parent, etc., hoping that doing so will bring guaranteed fair play to you, and the rest of the world, resulting in the 5-star career or life you want, is a mistake.

A TYPICAL SCENARIO

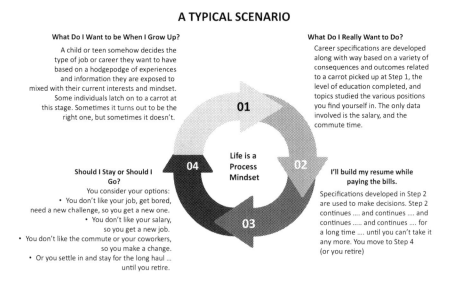

What Do I Want to be When I Grow Up?
A child or teen somehow decides the type of job or career they want to have based on a hodgepodge of experiences and information they are exposed to mixed with their current interests and mindset. Some individuals latch on to a carrot at this stage. Sometimes it turns out to be the right one, but sometimes it doesn't.

What Do I Really Want to Do?
Career specifications are developed along with way based on a variety of consequences and outcomes related to a carrot picked up at Step 1, the level of education completed, and topics studied the various positions you find yourself in. The only data involved is the salary, and the commute time.

Should I Stay or Should I Go?
You consider your options:
• You don't like your job, get bored, need a new challenge, so you get a new one.
• You don't like your salary, so you get a new job.
• You don't like the commute or your coworkers, so you make a change.
• Or you settle in and stay for the long haul ... until you retire.

I'll build my resume while paying the bills.
Specifications developed in Step 2 are used to make decisions. Step 2 continues .... and continues .... and continues ..... and continues .... for a long time .... until you can't take it any more. You move to Step 4 (or you retire)

01 02 03 04

Life is a Process Mindset

FIGURE 4.2
A typical scenario.

If that's your strategy, you're defining the 5-star career you want, and then waiting for someone else to come along and pave the way for you to have it. According to the proven science of quality management, that is a

TABLE 4.3

The Loosey-Goosey Career Manufacturing Process

My New Loosey-Goosey Career Manufacturing Process Our Motto: We Know Exactly What We Want!	
Step 1	We will focus on clearly defining our product. It's critical to know exactly what we want to manufacture.
Step 2	We will then focus all our time on hoping, asking, convincing, begging, and discussing what we need with other people and companies because until they give us that, we can't produce the product.
Step 3	If we get part of what we need, we'll give it a shot. (But we're all going to be resentful that Company A and B refused to give us what we asked for and therefore caused us to miss our target.)

flawed system. It will not produce the desired outcome. It would be like the loosey-goosey company shifting their strategy to the one in Table 4.3.

Regardless of the details of your story, your time bank is growing smaller every day. You are the manufacturer! You have the power to set the tone and control the factory floor. Understanding and embracing this reality is a key reason why philosophy and mindset, which together drive culture, are crucial elements in the science of quality management. If more individuals apply the science of quality management to their lives and careers, perhaps children will wake up in a culture that supports the ongoing production of a 5-star world.

NOT ALL PROCESSES ARE PURPOSEFUL AND SYSTEMATIC

In my book, *Six Sigma for Business Excellence: A Manager's Guide to Supervising Six Sigma Projects and Teams* (McGraw-Hill), I wrote an entire chapter on *process* without defining the term *process*. That's because, when applied to business, my intended readers understood the meaning of *process*. Industry managers have goals to achieve and outcomes to deliver. They inherently understand the need for some type of process, no matter how simple, to support and ensure success.

Imagine that a manager tasked to manufacture 5,000 perfect widgets within budget by the end of the month doesn't follow a purposeful and systematic process. Ultimately, she fails to achieve the goal. (Maybe this woman works for the loosey-goosey company.) In the wake of her failure, she looks at her boss, team, and customers, and says, "Well, it's a process, right? Live and learn." She would not come across as responsible, intelligent, driven, or motivated, right? Her boss would likely have serious concerns and think, "No wonder she couldn't deliver; perhaps I should find another manager?" A positive-thinking, motivated, responsible manager in the same scenario might feel horrible about failing and take it upon himself to figure out what the heck happened. He doesn't want to ever repeat this catastrophe! This is admirable. However, the science of quality management is about getting it right the first time. Neither of these managers are likely to achieve their widget-related goals if they don't understand the definition and power of process.

Having a long-term goal, following a process, and charting a plan does not lock a company or an individual into a never-ending commitment. Evaluation along the way is a key element of quality management. There is room for process improvement, course correction, and reevaluation of customer expectations. The trick is knowing what it all means and how it works together to keep a company, or a career, on a path to success. If a company does not identify a goal or vision, lacks a process, or follows an out-of-control, defective process, it will likely fail to produce a widget that consumers consider 5-star worthy.

The same is true for a career. If you're beginning to understand why making a commitment to quality and building a quality culture are needed to support the development of purposeful and systematic processes, it's time to clarify *process. Process* is defined as "a series of logically related activities or tasks (such as planning, production, or sales) performed together to produce a defined set of results." You can identify the various activities and tasks you spend your time on for the purpose, or hope, of producing a product (aka a 5-star career). You can then determine if those activities and tasks fit the formal definition of *process* (whose purpose is to produce defined results). You may operate so haphazardly that things don't work together to produce results, or maybe you haven't defined the result you're working toward. In that case, how can your activities and tasks work together to get that result? Again, this is at the heart of quality management and the message I hope to relay. We all execute various high-level and detailed process whether we realize it or not. The question is whether the resulting product is the one that you want.

High-level processes have associated detail processes that enable the successful delivery of outputs that ultimately pave the way for the delivery of the final product. Think of an assembly line that includes the completion of 20 processes; therefore, the high-level assembly process includes 20 steps. Similarly, the execution of the specific steps required to gain admission to medical school is an example of one of the detailed processes required for the high-level process for manufacturing a medical career. Later in the book, I'll use the assembly line to explain how processes are monitored and improved, including how quality is controlled when things go awry. However, first we'll explore how product specifications are defined, and how that impacts quality and drives customer satisfaction in both the manufacturing of a widget and a career.

KEY POINTS

1. Just as industry purposefully and systematically develops a product, you can consciously control, and therefore purposefully and systematically develop a career.
2. Many people make what seem to be well-thought-out, immediate career decisions with the assumption that making the right choice at that time will naturally lead to the next step, another weighty decision to make when the time comes. Unfortunately, next steps are often slow to come, or a decision that seemed right at the time was made in a vacuum or was supported by inaccurate assumptions.
3. If you commit to manufacturing a 5-star career, you must view yourself as the manufacturer who is 100% responsible for the quality of your career. This is one of the most difficult concepts to embrace.
4. The science of quality management has proven repeatedly over the last 100 years that believing in and valuing quality docs not make quality happen.
5. Quality must be designed into the system (remember systems exist whether we realize it or not) that generates the product and then purposefully managed. Ignoring this fact, being too busy to do it, or pushing the associated actions to the bottom of the priority list incurs a cost down the road.

6. I have no idea when, where, or how anything went wrong for you, but I know that you can find out and use that knowledge to finally manufacture a 5-star career.
7. Waiting to hand your power to a person, group, cause, boss, parent, etc., hoping that doing so will guarantee fair play, resulting in the 5-star career or life you want, is a mistake.
8. Regardless of the details of your story, your time bank is growing smaller every day. You are the manufacturer! You have the power to set the tone and control the factory floor.

BIBLIOGRAPHY

Dale Carnegie. *How to Win Friends and Influence People* (Pocket Books, 1998).

Mihaly Csikszentmihalyi. *Flow: The Psychology of Optimal Experience* (Harper Perennial Modern Classics, 2008).

Penelope Przekop. *Six Sigma for Business Management: A Manager's Guide to Supervising Six Sigma Projects and Teams* (McGraw-Hill, 2005).

Wayne W. Dyer. *Your Erroneous Zones: Step-by-Step Advice for Escaping the Trap of Negative Thinking and Taking Control of Your Life* (William Morrow Paperbacks, 2001).

5

We're All Customers

"Quality is defined by the satisfaction of the customers."

—W. Edwards Deming

Academic experts on the science of quality management as well as those who apply it daily have amassed irrefutable proof that the quality of a product or service is directly related to its ability to meet the intended need of the customer. The customer ultimately assigns value to the product. A widget deemed perfect by the manufacturer that fails to satisfy customers is far from perfect. In this case, the widgets sit on shelves while the company scrambles to stay afloat, perhaps at a loss to explain why something so wonderfully created isn't on every consumer's wish list. While knowing who the customer is may seem straightforward, it can get tricky in business and in life. On the job, employees and sometimes, entire companies can lose sight of their customers while focusing on their more immediate desire to satisfy their immediate supervisors, those who report to them, the team, their families, the finance department, their monthly bank account, etc. Those goals are important but can create a complex situation that ultimately produces a product that fails to satisfy the intended customer enough to warrant a 5-star review.

At the root of invention and innovation, you'll find those who set out to resolve a problem, whether it was specific to them or to others. The purpose of creating a new or revised product or service is to satisfy an existing or forecasted need or desire. In today's competitive world, the company that satisfies its customers to the greatest extent receives 5-star reviews. Companies often have large budgets dedicated to understanding the needs of their customers; this is a smart, common sense business

DOI: 10.4324/9780367855260-5

practice. In their search to define exactly what customers want, companies distribute surveys, evaluate online reviews, conduct complex market research projects, and more. They evaluate sales data to identify the best- and worst-selling products. They evaluate advertising, market variables, and purchasing trends. The purpose of these activities is to not only make the sale, but also inspire 5-star reviews..

If you're the manufacturer of your 5-star career, who's the customer? Who has it been all this time? *You* have always been the customer. There is no other nor will there ever be another. The career you have on any given day will qualify as 5-star when it meets the criteria that are most valuable to the authentic individual reading this sentence. This means that the career you are responsible for manufacturing will not be 5-star worthy until you not only clarify your own authentic needs and desires, but also determine why the career you have manufactured to date does not meet those specifications.

This brings us to the second of four concepts introduced in Chapter 1:

1. Life is not a process nor is your career. Your career is a *product* created by your process.
2. **Quality is defined by the customer; the quality of your product (career/life) is defined by you.**
3. Quality cannot be accurately rated or improved until it's defined.
4. You are 100% responsible for your product.

Accepting that you are the customer for your own career is not the easiest concept to digest. Two reasons for that are the following:

1. When asked to describe the job/career that you personally deem 5-star worthy (for you), the thought process tends to settle on a high-level response, which may also be an initial knee-jerk reaction. A few examples are:
    - My dream is to have a six-figure salary. Once I'm there, the rest will be gravy.
    - I don't ask for much. I just want a good-paying, steady job.
    - I want to be a surgeon!
    - All I've ever wanted is to be a teacher.

Realistically, there are people who set and achieve those goals and enjoy a 5-star career until the day they retire. However, if it were that simple across the board, the world would have millions more surgeons, teachers, and people with good-paying, steady work and six-figure salaries who wake up daily feeling that they are living their 5-star dream.

2. You were likely instructed from an early age to "do a good job," when completing chores, doing schoolwork, competing in athletics, writing reports, and the list goes on. Each of those activities was assigned to you by someone who expected it to be completed within a certain time and to the best of your ability. There's nothing wrong with that. Doing an excellent job is important! Submitting reports on time, correctly removing someone's appendix, operating the cash register properly, and accurately following a teaching syllabus are requirements of the job, and you should certainly execute them to the best of your ability. However, those are not a 5-star career, which is the final product you are manufacturing. Executing assigned tasks on time and to the best of your ability may be required steps in the manufacture of your 5-star career. However, overfocusing on their delivery with no thought to the larger picture, or believing that they *are* the big picture, will slow down the manufacture of your final product. Trust me I've seen people who delivered excellent work on time for years continue to do that for years while a colleague who wasn't as detail oriented and turned things in late a few times was promoted two levels during the same time period, all to the astonishment of the perfectionist. How can that happen? That's a complex question that you nor I may ever be able to answer because we don't know all the facts. What you can do is make sure that you're not the one who ends up turning in perfect assignments year after year wondering why nothing is changing in your life. Forget about the other guy. What happens to him is not within your scope; it's a waste of your time.

So, if you shouldn't overfocus on the task at hand, what should you do? That stuff still has to get done, right? Keep reading and all will be revealed. For now, let's recall that a quality management systems approach starts at the top. Tasks like those above, although important, fall much lower in that system hierarchy. It's all about focusing on all of these aspects following a priority perspective that will ultimately lead to the manufacture of the 5-star widget (or career). Table 5.1 provides a simplified industry example, again using the assembly line.

TABLE 5.1

Example of Top-Down Quality Management Systems Approach

Keys Steps for Process Development within a Quality System	Systems Levels (The System Is Built/Created from the Top Down)	Example/Notes
1.	Corporate quality policy	The CEO announces the corporate-wide policy that expresses the company's philosophy and shared commitment to quality that will be upheld as they develop and market products. The CEO focuses daily on ensuring that he demonstrates behaviors that support the quality policy.
2.	Other corporate policies	Corporate policies that support the quality policy are documented to serve as more specific guiding policies that may be required. Examples are employee corporate conduct and anti-trust policies.
3.	High-level processes	The company designs and documents the primary high-level process required to produce a final product that meets the specifications. One of those high-level processes is the assembly line discussed earlier. It includes 20 steps.
4.	Supporting processes	Each of the 20 required steps is complex enough to require separate documented process steps. These are developed.

The example in Table 5.1 is intended to support the point that doing an excellent job on any given task is certainly important; however, believing that's all there is to it is short sighted. You are the key customer for the product, which is *not* a task. It is a career. The quality rating that your boss, team, parents, kids, spouse, friends, business colleagues, or anyone else gives the tasks you complete or the report you write today is not your career rating. For some, this concept is easier understood than applied. This is why you could have a six-figure salary in a 3-star career, or a 2-star career that your spouse, parents, or kids may take pride in. Your boss may even believe that you are a 5-star-rated employee, yet to you, it's all still a 3-star career. A 5-star career is the product/outcome you want, and you are the customer of that product. You are to define it, evaluate it, improve it, and provide it back to yourself. There are people who don't care about the end/key customer. If the boss is happy, they feel successful. That's what I call a short-term win. The science behind quality management is not about the short-term – it's about strategy. It's about doing it right from the start so that you can get it right at the end. And that's what we should all want for ourselves. I won't lie. It takes patience and discipline, and it's harder for some of us.

COASTING WON'T TAKE YOU FAR

When purchasing a used, $1,000 car, my guess is that you realize that you're not driving off the lot with a $60,000 vehicle. However, you have expectations about the car's value based on the information you have and the sticker price. Maybe the $1,000 car is a 5-star rated vehicle originally purchased 20 years ago by a 65-year-old woman who, unfortunately, had a stroke the next day. She was never able to drive the car and it's been parked in her garage since that fateful day. Her son, who is now a retired mechanic, faithfully gave it a full-service tune up every 18 months. Based on this information, you're thrilled and buy the car. You feel secure about the car's value based on its history along with the make, model, price, etc. After driving it for a couple of months, you may even be inspired to write an online review of the car dealership, including a 5-star rating. However, if the car has several issues by that time, you may be frustrated. When that happens, you make several attempts to discuss the car and its history with the salesman. When that doesn't work out, you call the owner and leave a message. You hear crickets. You conclude that the car was falsely advertised; the dude just wanted to make a sale! You grab your laptop, determined not to let this happen to anyone else. In this scenario, the dealership gets a 1-star rating, which you feel is generous. The car dealership sold a product and provided a service that did not meet your expectations. Businesses like this rarely thrive, and if they do, they rarely grow. The 1-star car dealership owner has never heard of the science of quality management. He learned all about cars and how to sell them from his grandfather, who started the business. The dealership delivered a product that did not meet customer expectations, among other things. If they recognized and were concerned about the experiences of their customers, they would study their reviews to better understand what went wrong. They would also learn about quality management and how they can apply the concepts to their business. This could turn their business around; otherwise, becoming a 5-star rated business may turn into an endless uphill battle. Cars will sell now and then. Employees will be paid. The company will coast along; that's the type of company it will be, until the owner is ready to close the doors for the last time.

Careers can also coast along, failing to grow. If coasting satisfies you, that's fine. Maybe whatever you're doing is already a 5-star career. In that case, you're not coasting, you're enjoying! This is about what satisfies you, not me, not your colleagues or siblings. You're in the business of manufacturing various products, one of which is your career. If you know you're coasting along at 3 stars, and prefer not to, you have a phenomenal advantage! You are not only the manufacturer; you are also the customer. Phenomenal products, innovation, inventions, businesses, and services are born every day because someone recognizes that they need something that no one can provide them; it is not available to them. When faced with this gap, they have a lightbulb moment. They realize that they can create it; after all they have the best possible insight into what will satisfy the customer. They can be both the customer and the manufacturer. Wow! There's no better situation and it's yours. When it comes to manufacturing a 5-star career, it's easy to rush through it and state all the things that most people may agree on as a high-quality career. Things like a good salary, a good boss, a wonderful place to work, good vacations, and benefits. If it were that simple, a lot more of us would be satisfied. Sure, those things are usually quite important in a general sense, but you must ask yourself what you really want as an individual. Once you know what you want in a more detailed sense, you can begin to decipher why you don't have it yet.

HORSES HAVE EXCELLENT FOCUS

When it comes to the work that you do, like many people, including me, you may have developed a focus that moves you along like a horse follows a carrot. This may have resulted from years of hearing that you should "do a good job," or something else that influenced you in an even more powerful way. When a horse hungers for a carrot and therefore follows it, doing so prevents the animal from being distracted by other sensory input which can slow progress or influence movement in a direction of its choosing. It seems like a great idea, for someone who wants to get a horse from point a to point b. However, if the horse is moving in a less than ideal direction, such as toward a cliff, what then? The animal will walk on and on believing that he's on the right road and that he will soon get that carrot. The reality is that he never really had a choice. He was not following his own path after all, and the carrot he believed would satisfy him is only going to lead him off a cliff. It sounds horrible on multiple levels. The horse did all that work for nothing. He was goal oriented and focused. Yet, something went terribly wrong.

We've all heard that being goal oriented is a good thing, and I agree. Let's face it, what draws your mental, emotional, and physical attention (which means focus) daily molds most of your goals. A focus is there (a carrot), guiding your perceptions and actions. It may seem as if I'm referring to goals, but I'm not. A goal is different than focus. One can focus on a goal, sure, but that's not the type of focus I'm referring to here. Many excellent books have been written about how to retain focus and avoid distractions. The overall productivity and the completion of our daily work absolutely require focus. If you don't produce a report that's due by end of week because you've deemed it unimportant, or decide that focusing on the road isn't required when you're a truckdriver, you're going to struggle.

On the other hand, if that is happening to an extreme, the key question is: why are you doing tasks that you consider such low priority? What do you prefer to do with all your time? These types of questions hold powerful customer information. We'll discuss that more in Chapter 9. The amazing news is that the science of quality management teaches us how to create a system that guides us to focus *starting* with the big picture, then drill down, attending to the details in a way that supports the big picture and ultimately delivers our final product. Perhaps this appealed to me from the start because I lacked a solid structure as a kid. Structure is a many-layered topic, just like quality. That structure is your system. It's always there; it just may be weak, flawed, or slippery. As much as I wanted it to be true, I learned that finishing perfect reports on time, purchasing a house, landing a fantastic job, or starting a business is not enough to create a deep and unwavering structure (aka system) that allows you to finally walk on solid ground toward your chosen destination. You can have all that see glimpses of your desired destination, yet still be walking on the edge of a cliff. One change of the wind and you're in a free fall, whether that fall is short or long. That's what happened to me, and I'll share that story soon. I followed a few different carrots for years and hope to snap anyone I can possibly can out of that trance.

When it comes to your career, has your focus been unwavering or has it constantly shifted? Many people focus on time management or completing their tasks on time, every time. Some people focus on the people around them; they believe networking is the answer, not the content of their reports. There are numerous elements of a career that one could choose to focus on, believing that is what will lead to a 5-star career. I hope to relay how a focus on quality systems and the elements that contribute to such a system are key to manufacturing your 5-star career. The level of personal difficulty in shifting to a focus on these elements will vary. It wasn't easy for me. My dad used to tell me to smile until I felt like it. I quickly realized that the act of smiling did make me feel better. Now I know that smiling triggers your body to release feel-good enzymes.

I also learned in a training course that if you stand up, feet slightly apart, hands on hips, chin up, for a few minutes, you'll feel oddly more confident. We were asked to stand up and try it. It worked for me and I was impressed. Of course, that's not to say that all those things that wipe your smile away should be brushed under the rug, or that you should get into your confidence stance to help you ignore that you're bleeding and need to call 911. However, sometimes to grow, we need to actively choose to do things that feel unnatural. Things that feel oddly wrong when we know they're right. It could be as simple as turning on video in Zoom calls or something much more challenging. I learned that comfort is not always a good thing. I'm betting that you're familiar with the comfort zone. Sometimes we must establish a new comfort zone and getting there isn't all smooth sailing. Whether it's hitting the video button on Zoom, smiling when we don't feel like it, public speaking, an uncomfortable conversation to be had, a truth to face, or a 3-star career to step away from, there will always be bumps in the road. If you can't get past them, you'll never find out what's waiting around the next bend.

DON'T BE AFRAID TO SHOW YOUR FACE

Throughout my early career, I was good at recognizing comfort zones that I needed to move out of such as public speaking, managing others, or having to relay news that wasn't particularly welcome. However, there was one comfort zone that I was stuck in like the Hubba Bubba gum that, every now and then (for some reason), used to get stuck in my thick hair as a kid, usually after I had spent a couple of years letting my hair grow. My choices were to:

1. Ignore it, knowing that others may be able to see it and that would be weird. Even if no one noticed it, I would know it was there. I'd be uncomfortable all the time.
2. Cut it off and lose something I loved.
3. Or face the truly painful process of removing it. (Hopefully, there's an easier way to remove gum from hair now.)

In my early career, I chose the first solution to deal with the difficulty level I faced when considering how I could move beyond my particularly sticky comfort zone. There was a long stretch of time when I believed that if I pushed myself out of every other comfort zone I could think of, keeping that one would be okay. What I didn't realize was that a comfort zone should *be* comfortable. If it's not, then you likely do need to get out!

While going through two executive leadership programs that Johnson & Johnson selected me to attend (a big deal for me at the time), I found myself in a scenario where I couldn't deny that I was hiding a huge chunk of myself because I believed that it was the flawed part. The only way I had felt somewhat comfortable for years was to push what I thought was the broken, dysfunctional piece of myself into some sort of box and hide it away. I found comfort in knowing that there was a box, what was in it, and that the lid was tightly closed, but like the gum, I couldn't help but wonder if anyone else could see it. I thought that if I could get away with that, I could eventually have a 5-star matching life and career! It was working, Johnson & Johnson had chosen me out of hundreds of directors to attend not one but two special career development programs. I was so happy!

As I said, there turned out to be a kink that I didn't expect. One of the programs was all about authentic women's leadership, which posed a problem for me. How could I ever be an authentic leader when I had essentially shut down a major part of myself? To make matters worse, in many ways, the part in the box was the *most* authentic part of who I am, the person I didn't want to ever have to be again.

The trouble started on day two. The 15 or so women in attendance, all from Fortune 50 companies, were asked to arrange our chairs in a circle. First, we were asked to close our eyes and think way back, as far as we could recall to our early childhood. Once there we were asked to concentrate on the sights and sounds that we associated with our childhood. I saw my early childhood home but the images in my memory were in black and white, like the television we had. All I could hear was my mother screaming. All I could feel were my tiny fingers wiping away her tears in between the screaming. As an adult, I knew that those fingers were invisible to her. I felt claustrophobic. I opened my eyes before the others. Then, we were asked to take turns telling the group about our childhood for 10 or 15 minutes, particularly related to what we learned from our parents and the environment that they had created for us. As each accomplished woman (who all seemed to be inspired about being as authentic as possible) shared their stories of growing up, I became quite distressed. While every story wasn't overflowing with rainbows and butterflies, they all sounded great to me. They seemed healthy. They were aligned with what I was successfully providing for my children, along with my husband. Whether their parents were still married or had divorced, it was clear that each woman had some sort of structure holding her in place. My heart began to thud in my head. I couldn't seem to coach myself out of feeling upset. Emotionally, I kept trying to push the lid of my secret box down tight, but it seemed to keep popping off. I went to the restroom and wanted to stay there. Then I told myself that I was being silly. I had to go back. By the time I returned to my chair, I was in a tiny tailspin that didn't stop for several years. In fact, it grew into a tornado by 2012. Sitting in a circle with those women who were supposed to be my colleagues, my fellow golden girls, I didn't want to share any of my childhood. I wanted to lie and wondered if I should just make something up. After all, I had no obligation to tell them my personal history.

My chest literally hurt as I tried to decide what to say about my childhood, how I could be authentic and speak the truth. Listening to their stories confirmed how unusual mine was, at least in the present group. For the most part, they all described traditional upbringings with parents who believed in them, despite a divorce here, and hardship there. I wondered if anyone was lying, leaving out shocking details they preferred not to share. However, each woman seemed composed and confident. They were young directors and vice presidents ready to take on the corporate world. Lots of smiles. That's what I was, too, right? I sat there hoping that if I didn't verbalize my past, I could pretend it never happened, which is what I usually did. When my turn came, I didn't lie but I skimmed over the meat and heart of my story, of myself, smiled, and gave the floor to the next successful woman. I learned in the following years that all the parts of yourself that you may not like or that you'd like to hide can never truly be hidden. They snake their way into the forefront of your life in insidious ways that continue to trip you up and hold you back.

The program about authentic leadership taught me that I wanted to be and could be a truly authentic leader, but that was not at all what I had been doing. I stewed over this, the tiny whirlwind in motion, for a couple of years. I grew less and less comfortable with who I had become, right up to the day that I was called into a big conference room and told that I would no longer be needed by Johnson & Johnson. The reason was simply the budget. It didn't matter that my employee ratings had been in the high band every year, that the company sent me to special programs, how many potential new leaders that I had brought into the company, or what I had accomplished personally, or what I'd inspired my team to accomplish. Please sign here and there's the door. Best of luck!

WE ALL START SOMEWHERE

The place in which a story unfolds plays a pivotal role. I grew up in Shreveport, Louisiana, a city of about 200,000 that's just a couple of hours east of Dallas. In a 1961 study, Wilbur Zelinsky, an American cultural geographer and professor emeritus at Pennsylvania State University, delineated the Bible Belt as a region of the Southern United States in which socially conservative evangelical Protestantism plays a strong role in society and politics, and church attendance across the denominations is generally higher than the nation's average. Since the 1980s, the Bible Belt has been sliced and diced in various ways; however, a study commissioned by the American Bible Society to survey the importance of the Bible in the metropolitan areas of the United States revealed that Shreveport ranked as the second most "Bible-minded" city. The report was based on 42,855 interviews conducted between 2005 and 2012. As recently as 2014, results of a study conducted by Pew Forum showed that Louisiana and Alabama were the only US states in which over 90% of respondents stated that religion is "Very important" in their lives. By the time we grew up, my bother John and I agreed that Shreveport was most certainly the buckle of the Bible Belt.

If surveyed in 1977, today, or on any day in between, neither the American Bible Society nor any other society could offer a survey choice that would accurately relay how important religion, specifically Jesus, is in my mother's life. As you can imagine, religious beliefs meshed with mental illness seamlessly blend into the culture of Shreveport easier than just about anywhere else on God's green Earth. It is what it is, as they say. After digesting that bit of information, you may be surprised to know that my mother was a successful entrepreneur in 1977, which was highly forward thinking, liberal, if you will, at that time. Her creative career as a high-end interior designer and her passion for Jesus in a city teeming with wealthy, religious housewives who saw my mother as a hero worked beautifully in her favor. A free-standing office building in what was considered "the part of town where rich people lived" housed her interior design firm. We called it *the shop*. It had a fabulous showroom, a private office for her, and a large area, which would be described today as an open-concept space, with seating for six employees. There was a wall with floor-to-ceiling hooks on which at least a hundred fabric books hung, and a large square island used by the designers was the room's centerpiece. My mom's designers often stood around the island in their designer outfits, discussing design concepts with swatches and sketches spread out before them in a feast of colors and patterns. I saw these women as successful, smart, beautiful creatures entitled to do whatever they wanted to do with time that they owned. I never once thought that there was anything unusual about that; it made sense to me. The shop also included a smaller area off to the side for my mom's secretary, Diane. The lighting was not quite as bright there. It seemed like Diane was always sitting there typing on the giant electric typewriter in the middle of her industrial black desk that reminded me of an anchor. She was one of the kindest women I knew. She gave me a feeling of *mother* that drew me to her and added to my emotional confusion a few years later when my dad discovered that Diana was embezzling money from the firm. I was heartbroken, mainly because I wouldn't see Diana anymore.

The shop included a kitchenette, bathroom, and storage room. Jane Hall Interior Design had opened a couple of years earlier, after my mother developed a professional design reputation at the most exclusive design firm in Shreveport. She has always loved telling the miraculous story of how Jesus suddenly told her immediately to "go to the bank." She did as she was told and, lo and behold, someone at the bank handed her thousands of dollars to start her business. In fact, this didn't just happen once, according to my mother, eyes sparkling. It happened three times in a row until she had the *exact* amount of money needed to execute her plans. Recently my dad clarified that he went to the bank and took out a loan.

Before the *shop*, my grandfather, dad, and a family friend worked to renovate the first location of my mother's design firm every weekend for at least six months. John and I were required to tag along; we were too young to be left at home. I was about 11. I thought that we simply weren't trusted suddenly, since we'd been left home alone tons of times. We were latchkey kids. In the early 1970s, as first and second graders, we walked home from school and stayed there alone for an hour or two until our dad came home from his job as a high school teacher. Then there were the years that I stayed home along during June and July, John went to a special private school that only had a short summer break in August. Regardless of all that, we had to go. My brother helped a lot with the renovations and subsequently grew up to be quite handy around the house. I was expected to stay out of the way and entertain myself in some way that did not involve hammering a nail or getting dirty doing anything too strenuous. I knew it was because I was a girl, but I didn't care; I wasn't interested in construction or loud banging. I often read. Sometimes I brought a tiny white portable television we owned. It has an eight inch black and white screen. It could pick up the whopping three channels we had at the time. John and I spent many hours there during that time. Sometimes we came up with things that we could do together. Once we climbed onto the roof and walked around; it felt like an adventure. John's grand plan was to jump off and out into a giant pile of leaves in the yard below. He successfully executed this risky jump repeatedly, but I was afraid. After trying to convince me for quite a while he decided to simply push me off. I remember feeling betrayed, as if he was trying to kill me; I told myself that he just wanted me to understand that it was fun. I didn't land anywhere near the leaf pile, and it was not fun. It frightened me, hurt my pride, and several parts of my small body. I tried not to cry and didn't tell on him. I never told anyone. I didn't want to cause John any trouble; we both already had more than enough.

As a role model, the single, greatest thing that my mother gave me was her example of being a woman entrepreneur. Most of the moms I knew still stayed in the home; it was the 1970s and 1980s and we lived in the buckle of the Bible Belt. Any women who worked were nurses, teachers, or secretaries, all admirable professions, of course. Because of my mother's example, my vision of a career had no limits. I wanted it to be spectacularly unique and adventurous in a creative or intellectual way, although I had no idea what that would look like. When I was about 12, my mother and I were alone at the shop one day. It was one of those tween moments when I felt a flashing zing of being my own person. I stood in the center of my career hero's amazing office building bursting with drive and a passion for achievement, leadership, and knowledge. I announced to her, "I love sitting at Diane's desk. When I grow up, I want to have a big desk!" I wanted to be an expert at something, like my mom. Important, like my mom. Successful, like her. She looked at me as if I were a cute, little puppy, patted my head, and said, "Maybe someday you can be a secretary like Diane." My heart sank. Then I felt bad about my heart sinking. I loved Diane but I didn't want to be the secretary. I wanted to be the boss. Apparently, my mom knew something about me that I didn't. Despite the zing, I still believed my mom was always right and that she knew just about everything. I felt confused about the zing, about thinking that maybe I could be as great as she was. That's the first time I recall a crack forming in my belief that I could do whatever I set out to do. Some call those moments growing up. Some call them moments of truth, times when we realize how small we are. There's a lot of unavoidable coming-of-age pain mixed in with the electricity it can bring. That's why it's a category for books and movie. Many of us began, even as kids, to lose sight of our belief that we're just as capable as everyone else in the room; that we're exceptionally capable of meeting our full potential; that we can make our dreams come true, regardless of mistakes and missteps along the way; and that we should never believe those who underestimate us.

WHAT DO YOU WANT?

I'm sharing bits and pieces of my story for a reason; you have your own. Yours may be closer to the stories those women told in that circle that made me squirm (I hope so), or it could make mine look like a day at Disney World (I hope not). However, whether your story is better or worse than mine or anyone else's, it belongs to you. For that reason, it's both precious and priceless, teaming with the gold that created who you are. Rather than letting it possibly hold you back in any way, you can find the gold. Once you do, you'll know that you can afford to be authentic.

If you already have the career or job that you truly want, that's great. I grew up with an urge to constantly evolve; the thought of evolving, of things changing, gave me hope. There are numerous ways to evolve, one of which is through the work that we do every day, the activities to which we give so much of our limited time. Perhaps my urge to evolve is genetic. Perhaps it developed due to the dysfunctional environment I had to navigate as a child. Even now, I'm uncomfortable with the idea of waking up in five years in the same place doing the same thing I'm doing today; I've had to learn to accept consistency in several areas of my life. I grew up without consistency and adapted to that as best I could. I learned how to be as comfortable as possible faced with constant change. I settled for comfort zones that weren't comfortable. You may find comfort in extreme consistency and struggle with change. If so, your 5-star career may include consistency as a primary specification, or maybe consistency is a comfort zone that holds you back from the 5-star career you truly want. There are deeply layered reasons why each one of us has or will have a 5-star career specification list that is unique to us. The point is that you are the only one who can make that list for yourself. You're the customer. You are powerful.

KEY POINTS

1. The quality of a product or service is directly related to its ability to satisfy the intended customer. The customer ultimately assigns value to the product. A widget deemed perfect by the manufacturer that fails to satisfy customers is far from perfect.
2. *You* have always been the customer. There is no other nor will there ever be another.
3. Submitting reports on time, correctly removing someone's appendix, operating the cash register properly, and accurately following a teaching syllabus are requirements of the job and you should certainly execute them to the best of your ability. However, those are not a 5-star career, which is the final product you are manufacturing.
4. Quality management is not about the short-term – it's about strategy. It's about doing it right from the start so that you can get it right at

the end. And that's what we should all want for ourselves. I won't lie. It takes patience and discipline, and it's harder for some of us.

5. If coasting satisfies you, that's fine. Maybe whatever you're doing is already a 5-star career. In that case, you're not coasting, you're enjoying!

6. The science of quality management teaches us how to create a system that guides us to focus starting with the big picture, then drill down, attending to the details in a way that supports the big picture and ultimately delivers our final product.

7. There are numerous elements of a career that one can choose to focus on, believing that is what will lead to a 5-star career. I hope to relay how a focus on quality systems and the elements that contribute to such a system is key to manufacturing your 5-star career. The level of personal difficulty in shifting to a focus on these elements will vary.

8. It doesn't matter if your story is better or worse than mine or anyone else's; it belongs to you. For that reason, it's both precious and priceless, teaming with the gold that created who you are. Rather than letting it possibly hold you back in any way, you can find the gold. Once you do, you'll know that you can afford to be authentic.

6

Customers Have Problems

"If I had asked people what they wanted, they would have said faster horses."

—Henry Ford

Products are specific to an intended customer. Consider what that means and why it matters so much. We know that once a widget is purchased by the intended customer, that person will assign a quality value to it based on their satisfaction with it. That could be in an online review or simply in their head. For this reason, manufacturers need specifics. Companies can't make broad assumptions about what customers may want or need. Consider a company that manufactures products such as hairbrushes, clothing, and desks. These are all examples of products that you can find anywhere, just like companies can find people who will accept a paycheck anywhere and you can find a job anywhere if you literally have zero concerns about the details. If you don't believe me, binge watch Discovery Channels' *Dirty Jobs* with Mike Rowe. So why don't we make it easy by hiring anyone who is human, buying the first hairbrush we see, and taking any possible job we can get. (Sometimes, these things happen but it's not usually the preference.) If you want to follow the be-satisfied-with-anything approach, that's fine, but you don't have to do that. It's okay if you prefer not to work with Mike Rowe. For some people, this is a no brainer; for others, it's not so simple. It's important to know as you set out to clarify what it is that you do want.

According to Rocky, if we continue to get back up and try again, we are winners. That worked well for Rocky because he knew exactly what he wanted. He ultimately manufactured the win he desired by taking

DOI: 10.4324/9780367855260-6

responsibility and accepting the value of a systems approach to training. Our younger daughter is a division 1 track and field athlete at Stanford University. Growing up, her initial athletic focus was basketball. After playing competitively for 3 or 4 years, her 11-year-old intuition led her to share the following conclusions when her team lost. With tears in her gigantic blue eyes, she passionately expressed her deep frustration:

- It was the coach's fault. He should have sent in the best two players during the second quarter! He wasn't paying attention in the first quarter. When I tried to tell him, he yelled at me to sit down. I was trying to help!
- I did my best. I worked so hard! The point guard was all over the place. She does that all the time. If the coach would just tell her to stop doing that, and pass the ball to me, we would win every time.
- They don't pass the ball to me enough. They hog the ball! Why would they do that if the goal is to win? Why doesn't somebody explain that to them?
- The other team didn't play fair! Even the coach knows it. Someone should complain. It's not fair!

After many years, tears, lessons, and demanding work, she graduated from high school with three Pennsylvania State High Jump Championship medals, and a rock-solid understanding that conclusions or solutions that are the most intuitive to you at any given time are not always the right ones, and even when they are, they may not be where you need to focus.

Intuitive people can understand something immediately, without the need for conscious reasoning. Well, guess what? We all experience intuition, even 11-year-olds; however, that doesn't mean we're always right, or that our conclusions or solutions are appropriate. *They* say to "trust your intuition" and I generally agree, but intuition is situational. If your intuition tells you that someone is about to punch you, run or brace yourself. If your intuition tells you that you're destined to be a billionaire and that you just need to wait for it to happen, that may not be the wisest approach. I bet you know someone who considers themselves to be highly intuitive; however, you happen to know that they end up being wrong 80% of the time. This is yet another example of how this giant world we live in is a system that neither you, nor anyone else, will ever, ever, be able to control. If an ant crawls into your home, would you recommend that it spend years of agony trying to understand and control what is happening there? You know that controlling your home is not an available option to this tiny ant, and that's okay. Instead, he should focus on understanding ant culture, his army, what he can do best there, and get to it. (Although I do love movies like *A Bug's Life* and *Antz*. They relay great messages. Those messages, however, do not include that an ant can control the giant fuzziness surrounding him.)

Note: ants and people should absolutely be involved and support global and local causes and movements important to them. The focus here is on understanding how you can follow the science of quality management to manufacture a highly specific product for which you are the *only* customer. Supporting and contributing to a shared cause you care deeply about may be included in the life and/or career that you deem 5-star worthy.

The ant could go on and on about how the man removed that chunk of food he was planning to grab because the queen is hungry. "If that giant creature just left it there, we could all be healthier this week! He couldn't possibly have a good reason to move it from that spot. We work so hard. It's so unfair!" Do the ant's lament, and our, then 11-year-old, daughter's highly intuitive solutions remind you of the following, by any chance?

- My boss was at fault. She should have done this or that. She wasn't paying attention in that meeting! When I tried to alert her, she frowned at me right in front of everyone. I was trying to help.
- I did my best. I worked so hard. My co-worker was nowhere to be found, as usual. If our boss would just tell him to cut it out, and work with me, we would be on time every month.
- My coworkers don't collaborate with me like they should because they're glory hounds.
- The other department is filled with people who will walk all over anyone to get ahead. The management knows it, and nobody does anything about it. It's incredibly unfair!

MOVIES ONLY LAST 90 MINUTES

The scenario in which a person wakes up, declares that it is "the first day of the rest of my life," and successfully applies advice they just read in a book to their career or life, is one of three things:

1) A rare exception, rather than the rule.
2) A scenario involving a person who is likely doing well by their own standards but is dissatisfied with a specific issue *and* the book they read is specifically about that issue. For example, perhaps it's Donna. She's happy and rates her career at 4.75 stars. However, she decides that she wants to ensure that her staff find her approachable. She knows that she has naturally severe features. She's happy with her physical attributes but maybe there's something she can do or learn to help her remember to physically smile when she's smiling on the inside. So, she finds a highly rated book titled *Smile More and They Will Come into Your office*. Bam! (What you just read is also an example of quality control, which will be covered later.)
3) The plot of a movie that is *not* based on a true story.

On the other hand, like me, you may have read one or more helpful books, excited to immediately execute the tips and advice, only to find that it's not quite that easy. Let's say the advice is to "Be Positive!" Okay, wow, that sounds so easy! If I'd only known that was my issue all this time! This changes everything! I just need to focus intensely on being positive. Nothing is going to distract me from my positive mindset, starting right now! I am positive. Go! A few days later, I'm smiling when I don't feel like smiling, knowing that part of the trick is not to acknowledge how I feel and keep smiling. Those amazing chemicals in my body are smiling, even if I don't feel like it right now because someone just ran into my car in a parking lot. Nevertheless, I get out of my car and smile. I keep smiling and smiling and smiling and smiling. A month later, I just can't do it anymore. What the heck is wrong with me? I feel like screaming!

Bottom line, you are a unique individual and a highly individual customer. You are special among your kind. One of the beautiful, amazing things about being human is that each one of us is unique among billions. Even if we smile and happy chemicals race through us, we are different, and many of the biological processes that make us different remain scientific mysteries. Some people have unique qualities that are highly visible; we label those lucky people as talented. Well, guess what? You're talented, whether you realize it or not. Whether it's obvious to a crowd, recognized within your family, known to yourself, or this is news to you. Discovering and embracing what your talents are is part of the research and analysis that I'll encourage you to do in the next few chapters.

ELITE ATHLETES APPLY QUALITY MANAGEMENT

It may be called training; however, the typical path people take to emerge as elite athletes follows the proven science of quality management. If it doesn't come inherently, along the way, elite athletes learn to accept ultimate responsibility for their performance. They also learn the value that a systems approach brings to their performance, one that includes the right philosophy, mindset, culture, processes, and more. They face the realization that it often takes more than getting back up a thousand times, and that sometimes the training they need feels counter-intuitive. While incredibly admirable, if an athlete gets back up after a devastating knock down, simply to repeat a flawed technique a thousand times, they're simply being repetitive. In fact, they're moving backwards. They are creating flawed muscle memory that makes every execution feel like intuition on steroids; no thinking required! This makes their progress much harder.

Smiling is admirable, too, but maintaining a grin 24/7 is not sustainable. Imagine getting back up a thousand times, all while smiling and focusing on positive thoughts, while unbeknownst to yourself, you're training yourself to fail. I'm exhausted just thinking about it. The point is to get back up and do it differently next time, every time, until you get it right. The only way to do that is to tease apart the elements of what occurred *that* exist within your scope of control. Then analyze the information to determine why the heck you ended up back on your butt.

Not accepting the philosophy and mindset discussed above can lead you to conduct your research and analysis incorrectly. Every time you get back up and blame the coach, you're handing over your power, and expecting the coach to not only understand its complexity. You're letting the coach make decisions on your behalf. If you're lucky, sure, you may get better, but how long is that going to take? Why are you wasting time? This is what Rocky ultimately realized (although the part about getting back up sticks with us just like the other advice sound bites listed in Chapter 4). We'll dive further into this process later.

Although we wear the jerseys, colors, and t-shirts, most of us are not elite athletes. We don't always have the luxury of a clear, precise goal to focus on during all our years of practice. We're customers who may or may not have a clue what we want, and yet our satisfaction defines the quality of the reward we ultimately will achieve. If you desire a 5-star career (or life) as passionately as an athlete wants to win, where does that leave you? At this very moment, it leaves you with the powerful opportunity to use the same principles proven in the manufacturing industry and used by athletes determined to leave the Olympic field feeling 5-star satisfaction, regardless of whether they take home the gold. Once I realized this, I couldn't believe that no one else had. Why didn't anyone tell me this stuff? A high school class on this topic may have changed my life. All I heard was do your best, offer to help, smile and work hard, and never give up … and in my case, don't sin, turn the other cheek, and rest assured that you are worthy because Jesus loves you, despite all the flaws you have. I believed every word.

It wasn't until I understood how quality is managed within a system that real sparks began to fly. I was blessed to feel loved by Jesus growing up, but that's not the point. Whether people want to accept it or not, or explain it away, believing that Jesus loves you is not always enough. I was taught that God created me so that I could worship him. Now, I suspect that my mother overfocused on that because she believed that I was created to worship her, and believing that about God made her feel better about her own need to be worshiped. Whoever and whatever gifted me with life should love me for who I am, not because I've arrived here to worship them.

A true artist loves her creation, not because she can use it to make a buck, but because it emerged from within her own being. It was somehow pulled out of her and now it stands before her, distinct and beautiful, something that can never be duplicated or recreated. It flourishes in its own space for its own purpose. If a time comes that it must distance itself to achieve that purpose, it carries a piece of its creator forward. Nothing is more precious than such a creation, especially when it carries humanity forward. That's the type of creation we are, you and me.

CUE THE ROCKY THEME

At some point in reading this book, some version of the following two thoughts may have popped into your head, "How can I do all this if I have no clue what I want?" and "How was I (or anyone else) supposed to know what I wanted when I was 18?" Those are great questions. The good news is that they will be addressed. Until we get to that page, be careful not to fall into the trap of making a knee-jerk conclusion that the science of quality management, and therefore, this book, adds unnecessary complexity to something simple. That it's busy work and will waste your time. As you and I grew up, a lot of what we learned or surmised about quality and how it's generated was incorrect. You, me, and everyone else launched into the adult workforce with many philosophies and perceptions that are difficult, but not impossible, to unlearn. Has anyone ever said something like this to you: "Your problem is that you'll never be satisfied; you don't even know what you want"? (By the way, if a manufacturer said that to their customers, they wouldn't be in business for too long.) Valuing what I have at any given moment is essential to a happy life, in my opinion. I love coming across posters and wall hangings that remind me to appreciate what's right in front of me. However, let's face it, if Rocky were easily satisfied with what he already had, he wouldn't be a champion nor would he have a statue at the foot of the Philadelphia Art Museum. Although a movie character, his dissatisfaction enabled the character to inspire millions of people.

How can a manufacturer satisfy customers who don't know what they want? Step 1 in the product development process (refer to Chapter 4, Figure 4.1) is about research and analysis. If customers always knew *exactly* what they wanted, Step 1 would be *Research*, or maybe *Ask the Customer*. Asking customers to send their specifications would do the trick. Research and analysis are part of the process because the manufacturer's role is to explore information about the intended customer (as a group) to generate conclusions about what they need or want, what draws their attention and why, what problems they have, what's already available that hasn't worked for them, etc. They rely on statistical methods to generate reliable data because no two people in the universe are the same. In the end, if the manufacturer hits the bullseye, customers will love the product, give it 5 stars on Amazon, tell their friends, and buy one for mom.

Cue the Rocky theme! Imagine your arms held high. You're running up, or jogging down, the steps of the Philadelphia Art Museum. Rocky's there, too, probably running up. He's dissatisfied but he knows what he wants and how to make it happen. You're dissatisfied. You may or may not know what you want but you are finding out a proven way to make it happen. My hope is that you start to feel that *zing* again, the exciting flicker of power that shot through you the time you realized that there's a big world out there, and that when you grow up, you can decide how to live. If you never felt that zing as a kid, I hope that you will at some turn of the page now. It's the soothing truth raining down in the best way. Hugs all around!

Okay, wait. Keep the music on but turn it down for a minute. In the spirit of full disclosure, I need to pause the party to say that time is required to digest all this information, embrace it, and figure out how to apply it within your personal scope of influence. My goal is to make it as easy as possible; that's all I can do within my scope/system of control. If you put in the time to get there, you'll realize that it was worth every moment, and even any tears it may have cost. I can say this with confidence because falling on your face in a quality management system includes a process for getting back up, identifying the root cause of the knockout, and determining the best possible action to correct that root cause as well as prevent it from happening again. Once you have that firmly in your back pocket, it's nirvana. I feel that way right now. I'm so excited that I could write all day and night, forever, if that's what it takes, to relay the value that's waiting for you. I'll be sad if I ever run into you somehow and find out that after you finished this book, you put it on a shelf, and kept smiling, and falling, and getting up, and hitting the ground, and smiling. I wasted a lot of time doing exactly that.

CUE THE DEMONS

Viewing ourselves as a unique creation chock full of value doesn't come easy to some of us due to our childhood experiences; those stressful, painful, pesky things that we had absolutely no control over happened when our brains were in high-speed growth mode. Full disclosure, as a child, I sensed that I had attributes that were unique to me; however, it was just a fluttering instinct that went without solid adult verification due to a family focus on surviving through a never-ending sea storm. The storm that was my mother essentially forced my brother, dad, and I to spend a tremendous amount of mental and emotional energy on keeping afloat. When trying to survive a never-ending storm, five-, six-, seven-year-old me tucked any suspicions I had about feeling unique away as if they were secret wishes rather than something true. Even within my own family, I sensed that there was something about me that was different from the other three. I didn't have a clue what it meant to be a real person, but I was becoming an expert at being part of a storm. At the time, I feared that believing I had a unique attribute, especially a positive one, meant that I had the audacity to think that I might be better than them in some way. Amidst the unhappiness, screaming, criticism, confusion, and drama *that* seemed like a horribly self-centered thought to entertain. What did such a bubbling, out of place feeling of individuality say about me? Who was I to feel that I might have any qualities to be proud of when everyone around me was miserable? I pushed all my self-centered thoughts as deeply as I could into the realm of magical secrets, the kind that turn into fantasies, dreams, and fairytales. I needed to be humble and supportive of a screaming, crying mom, a father struggling to cope the only way he knew how, and a brilliant, hyperactive brother who, at seven, was diagnosed with a learning disability. The best way to do that was to avoid adding a fully formed fourth person into the suffering mix, and instead intensely focus on who the other three were and how I could be of service. I had to cope, too. Yet I wanted to be unique, as if I weren't just part of a storm, just as intensely as I wanted my mother to love me.

When your mother is a storm, incapable of realizing that you're there, you begin to believe that anyone who knew how deeply you long to be an individual would conclude that you were arrogant, crazy, or silly. I didn't realize that I *was* a unique individual simply longing to be seen. In Sunday school, we learned about something called "the gifts of the Spirit." The adults there said that every single person has a gift. Although I'm not sure if I correctly interpreted what I heard during that lesson, it stuck in my brain like cement. This gave me hope! I equated gifts with talents. I wanted to be unique, and they were telling me that I had a talent! I just had to figure out what it was. At the time, I didn't associate having a gift or talent with things like singing, painting, or drawing. To me, it represented simply being able to do *something* incredibly well.

By the time I was in 7th grade (the year that God told my mother that he was going to kill off my dad to pave the way for her to be with our preacher), I had no doubt that I was dealing with a horrible flaw. I assumed that it was mine. I also realized that I wasn't smart enough to figure out *what* I was missing that had created this disaster. I blamed myself for the deficit, and for not being smart enough to figure out what it was and how to fix it. I began waking up every day as if encased in a dark, heavy cloud. I didn't realize that I was a child growing up in a dysfunctional home manipulated by mental illness. For at least two years, my mother had been warning me that I was surrounded by demons, all chomping at the bit to jump into me. New rules were established. We were no longer allowed to watch *Bewitched* or *I Dream of Jeannie*. We could only listen to the Christian music station. Those shows and that music would open us up, allowing all those lurking demons to run right in. She prayed for me in "deliverance," which was essentially exorcism. She called forth all kinds of demons; each was the spirit of something terrible like selfishness, arrogance, haughtiness, and even sexuality. I wasn't sure if they were leaving. Then I feared that they weren't even there, which meant that all those terrible *spirits* were descriptions of me.

I was eight years old in 1974, which was a few years earlier. A supernatural horror film, *The Exorcist*, was capturing audiences and awards, and influencing changes in the industry's rating system. The film follows the demonic possession of a 12-year-old and her mother's attempt to rescue her through an exorcism conducted by two Roman Catholic priests. It was also in 1974 that our preacher miraculously released my mother from an army of demons in the name of God. Following her supernatural experience, my mother became obsessed with the movement, that she said was sweeping through the country. She learned to conduct deliverance sessions, fell for the preacher, and was rarely home. When at home, she loved to share stories filled with details of sin, demons, twisting heads, and agonizing cries associated with gigantic tears, retching, and finally, joy. My brother and I both heard the stories; there was no escaping. I was the only one privy to the romantic angle. It went on and on and on. I moved between a state of terror and disgust. I didn't want to hear about the preacher. The day she told me that God had shared with her a plan involving the death of my dad, there was a shift. I finally began to tell her that I didn't want to hear about the preacher. Her consistent response was that I was selfish, that I should be willing to listen to her, and that I needed more deliverance.

My self-worth plummeted during my teen years. Everyone outside my own family seemed to have built-in navigation systems while I was stuck trying to read a map during a thunderstorm when I didn't even know where I was, or where I was supposed to go. The following list includes many of the accomplishments and facets of my life that contributed to a growing disconnect between what was happening around me and my internal philosophy and mindset:

- Placed in advance math (above the grade level range) in 5th and 6th grades.
- Won several 6th-grade competitions: Best Cornbread, Best Halloween Poster, Best Hat Design, Best Written Prayer submission for 6th-Grade Graduation, which I was awarded the honor of saying at the ceremony, my 6th-Grade Motto submission was selected and displayed at the graduation – "The Future is Ours to Create." (Yes, these were our big competitions; it was Louisiana in 1977.)
- Elected 7th-grade class president.
- Nabbed a leading role in a community play in 8th grade.
- Elected cheerleader by the student body throughout junior high and high school (after I graduated, they switched to using adult judges).
- Had no trouble getting a date.
- Completed nine years of tap-dancing classes.
- Placed in advanced classes throughout high school.
- Built a large repository of original poetry and other writings.
- Read more books than anyone I knew.
- Had many great friends who frequently included me in their social plans.
- Graduated from high school early to enter college.
- Became a runway model during my first year of college.
- Had my poetry published in a regional poetry magazine.
- Was awarded a full academic scholarship at the start of my sophomore year of college.
- Worked throughout college and had three jobs one summer.

The list above and the story leading to it serve to help demonstrate several of the concepts that have been covered including carrot following, how mindset evolves, how blind spots can hold us back, how what one person perceives as worth 5 stars can be worth 1 or 2 to the person next to them, and lastly, how the advice about not judging a book by its cover is spot on. Imagine a list of career accomplishments to date or the contents of your current resume. All that matters, all that should matter, is how you feel about what's included there. You can begin to understand how critical it is to know and accept yourself, determine what you truly want, be okay with acknowledging and sharing it with others, and begin making decisions that will take you down the right road, even if it means tossing a long-held carrot to the wind while others shake their heads in confusion. It ties in a bit with the concept that money doesn't guarantee happiness, that some people are miserable wherever they are, and that beauty is in the eye of the beholder. I've never been a cookie cutter person. I have a unique story and identity. Jumping straight into one of those common sense, cookie cutter solutions I read about during college was not a viable long-term solution for me. You weren't made with a cookie cutter either.

KEY POINTS

1. We all experience intuition, even 11-year-olds; however, that doesn't mean we're always right, or that our conclusions or solutions are appropriate.
2. *They* say to "trust your intuition" and I generally agree, but intuition is situational. If your intuition tells you that someone is about to punch you, run or brace yourself. If your intuition tells you that you're destined to be a billionaire and that you just need to wait for it to happen, that may not be the wisest approach.
3. You're talented, whether you realize it or not.
4. It may be called *training*; however, the typical path people take to emerge as elite athletes follows the proven science of quality management.
5. You are special among your kind. One of the beautiful, amazing things about being human is that each one of us is unique among billions. Even if we smile and happy chemicals race through us, we are different, and many of the biological processes that make us different are still scientific mysteries.

6. As you and I grew up, a lot of what we learned or surmised about quality and how it's generated was incorrect. You, me, and everyone else launched into the adult workforce with many philosophies and perceptions that are difficult, but not impossible, to unlearn.

7. Time is required to digest all this information, embrace it, and figure out how to apply it within your personal scope of influence. If you put in the time to get there, you'll realize that it was worth every moment, and even any tears it may have cost.

8. Falling on your face in a quality management system includes a process for getting back up, identifying the root cause of the knockout, and determining the best possible action to correct that root cause as well as prevent it from happening again. Once you have that firmly in your back pocket, it's nirvana.

7

We All Shop for the Big One

"Everybody is a genius. But if you judge a fish by its ability to climb a tree, it will live its whole life believing it is stupid."

—Albert Einstein

Human biology is an intricate assemblage of related units, many of which continue to remain a mystery. How can we possibly be simple creatures given the complexity required for each of us to be unique among millions, billions, or trillions? If most people were simple, we'd be more similar. Sure, we share the human condition, the body, the basic biology, all incredibly important things that connect us, yet drilling down into *exactly* who *you* are, you're alone in your exquisite individuality. That can feel amazing or isolating.

Every person who reads this book is amazing; accepting that and feeling it in your bones should be the goal. If you struggle with trusting that this should be a goal or have the opinion that achieving it will transform you into an arrogant or selfish individual, I hope to shift your mindset. I grew up in a culture constantly reminding me that I needed to be saved. Now I know that I have a free will, regardless of whether I believe that I need a savior in the context of Christianity. I'm an amazing creature with the tools required to live my best life; no other person or supernatural being can do that for me. I'm not a puppet on a string nor would I ever want to be. Puppets are utterly powerless. No matter what they do, who they please or entertain, what goals they meet with the help of the big guy holding the strings, they never *live* like we can.

We've all met people who seem to lack complexity; you get what you see. They're predictable. Rather than simple, these people may just be consistent, which offers a certain brand of trust to others. In Chapter 11, we'll explore why simple is not always easy, and the value consistency

DOI: 10.4324/9780367855260-7

brings to quality management. There are also people who enjoy letting others know just how simple they are, whether it's true or not. Given all the proven intricacies and remaining mysteries of human biology, research and analysis are required to verify the perceptions you have about your customer (yourself). If you happen to consider yourself a simple person for whom additional research may be uncalled for, good for you. In fact, you may already enjoy a 5-star career and are reading this book to check it out before gifting it to someone who you suspect may need it. That's wonderful! Theoretically, you'll breeze through the rest of the book, appreciate it, and gift it to others. However, if that's not the scenario, watch out for the trap of getting to the end of the book believing that you have a stellar plan based on what you know about your customer (you), only to find that it's not working. If that happens, I hope you'll consider that you may not be as simple as you thought and read this book again. If you commit now to diving in despite having confidence that you know yourself well enough, or if find yourself back here again, don't be surprised if you run into some unrecognized or untapped internal complexity. I'm using the term *untapped* because the hidden gems of authenticity are found in the intricate assemblage of who you are as an individual. That authenticity is the key to defining what quality means to you.

WHY ALL THE DISCONNECTS?

Given the information above, how can you know or accurately analyze any other human being except yourself? The field of psychology exists because it's challenging. In Chapter 1, you read about first impressions. First impressions are not all wrong. However, it is not within your scope to know the absolute, full, intricate story of any other person on the planet. But guess what, none of those people are the customer for the 5-star career that you hope to create. Isn't that a relief? Circling back to the details of my life that I shared in Chapter 6, consider the following questions:

1. Why was I unhappy despite obvious acceptance from my peers?
2. Why was I miserable no matter where I was?

3. Why might you be unhappy with your career despite having the salary you have worked towards for the last ten years?

4. Why do you end up miserable no matter where you're working?

5. Although you know that you have a lot to be thankful for, why do you still feel that somethings is *off*?

6. Why do you interview well but then can't seem to live up to the expectations?

7. Why do you always *seem* to be appreciated on the job but anytime you want or need to make a change, you can't seem to represent yourself well in interviews?

There are a lot of disconnects there! The list of my *positives* at the end of Chapter 6 seems to portray a young person who had unique, obvious-to-the-crowd qualities, and clear potential to develop into an intelligent, capable adult. By focusing on the disconnect between the list and the personal information I've shared, it becomes a powerful real-world example of the following quality management-related terms and concepts:

- **Product**: I had no clue what a 5-star anything meant to me in those moments of my life. My sense of self was severely underdeveloped for my age. Many of my decisions were based on what I perceived that my mother wanted, needed, or expected of me, which splashed out into how I operated with my peers. I was a kid, of course, but my sense of self continued to be tied to my mother long after it should have naturally separated and evolved. Sadly, my mother encouraged this due to having a personality disorder and mental illness. I thought that I had to create a product that my mother or peers would find satisfying. When I was praised or successful, the cycle grew stronger. I never realized that the customer was me; my deep dissatisfaction grew, and I blamed myself, deciding that something must surely be wrong with me.

- **Philosophy**: once I began to realize that a negative pattern was forming in my life, I was too ashamed and scared to be open about it or to ask for help. My overarching philosophy about life was trapped in a pattern that I couldn't seem to break. Although I was participating in activities for which I had genuine interest, I knew that wasn't enough, something continued to be *off*, yet I never told anyone. My deep concern for pleasing others tied me to a path

I couldn't escape. I was unhappy yet too afraid to be authentic or to explore what that meant or what it could look like. I kept most of my relationships at a specific level, even when I wanted more.

- **Blind spots**: I had a blind spot that kept me from seeing what was obvious to others. Although people clearly liked me according to the list I shared, it didn't seem to count. There was a deep emptiness inside me that felt ugly, cold, and angry. *That* felt more real to me than any of those other things. Any good feeling that I had was never strong enough to replace that darkness. I thought that my *list* might grow and eventually replace that darkness by creating a solid definition of who I was. When that wasn't working, I concluded that those things were not at all who I was; that I was simply skilled at showing people what they wanted to see. Afterall, hadn't I been doing that since I was born, not only for my mother, but also for my dad and brother? In my tiny, growing brain, I developed the sad belief that I was the only one who could add light to the storm. I was like an ant struggling to understand and manage an entire home.

    When I arrived at the age when we all become more self-aware, nothing was there for me to find, and my mother, free of her demons, was off to drive them out of everyone else, including me. As I sit here today, I know now that my mother selfishly took from me what she wanted and needed to survive until her miracle. Then she set out on a supernatural mission and left me behind, a tween looking inward to find nothing there. No cheerleading win, college scholarship, salary, title, or perfectly executed project at the largest company in the world can resolve an issue like that. I invented reasons why I was elected by my peers that supported my mindset and downplayed the significance or true meaning behind the data. Yes, those votes represented actual data from my personal story. Data does not lie. If I were only a being so deeply flawed that my own mother couldn't love me, anyone who *seemed* to like me must surely be mistaken. My mindset was sprinkled with blind spots that made the illogical seem logical.

- **Mindset**: my belief that I was *not* the person everyone thought that I was, and that anything outwardly positive or appreciated about me was some sort of role I was playing, slowed my growth. For many years, although I desperately wanted to, I feared that I was incapable of being anything different than what others wanted or were comfortable with. Now I realize that I was tossing my personal power into the trash; I needlessly gave it all away. I didn't know how or what to do to relive my feeling of being lonely in a crowd. I kept a smile on my face, did my best under the circumstances. I prayed for something or someone to come along to help me figure out what to do.

This mindset negatively impacted my more intimate relationships for years. The first time I fell in love, I was 17. I had no idea how love was best demonstrated or processed, but I fell into it and it was real. It was a new kind of sea storm, one that I could succumb to rather than be the one who remained steady. I could finally get lost in my own emotions. I could feel them all. I subconsciously hoped that he would be the one to finally prove I was worth loving. At the time, it seemed that we were there together, that he felt like I did. When it became too much for me, it seemed that he was the only one who could see me flailing, and therefore, the only who could pull me out. That desperation, coupled with my fear of emotional intimacy, was not a good recipe for developing a lasting bond. The relationship played a significant role in the path my life took. Years later, at 25, I set out to write my first novel, knowing that I needed to write about that relationship. By the time I finished the book, *Please Love Me*, five years later, I had gained new clarity. As I reflected on that relationship and how love hit me like a wound rather than a comfort, I tapped into an underlying need related to my mother. I began to realize that so many of the disconnects in my life were somehow tied to her. I still didn't understand why, or wasn't ready to digest the truth; however, my mindset began to inch toward a new direction.

WE ALL WANT THE BIG COOKIE

Now that you know that, just like snowflakes, you're exquisitely unique, I must remind you that you're still human. In Abraham Maslow's 1954 book *Motivation and Personality*, he expressed what has become a fundamental concept in modern psychology, referred to as Maslow's hierarchy of needs. Maslow's theory now widely accepted (although there are folks who challenge it), says that consciously or not, as a card-carrying member of the human species, we have a biological need for self-actualization. We carry a deep need to understand and achieve our full potential as unique individuals. Maslow theorized that there is a ladder of needs we must climb to reach self-actualization, which is the deepest possible level of satisfaction a human being can achieve. It is 5-star quality on steroids; who wouldn't want that? In Figure 7.1, you'll see Maslow's hierarchy of needs as described in his 1954 book *Motivation and Personality*. Interestingly, the proven science of quality management tells us how to manufacture 5-star quality, regardless of what that product may be. This is a win-win.

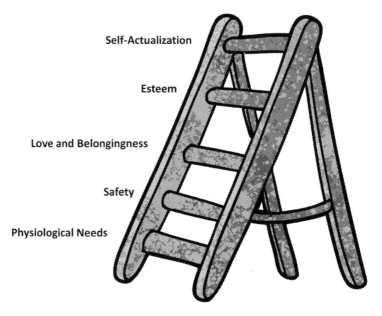

FIGURE 7.1
Maslow's hierarchy of needs (i.e., the ladder).

Maslow's hierarchy has been applied to all kinds of scenarios including employee engagement in the workplace. Good leaders often seek to understand what motivates their employees as a way to engage them in the work. This helps to drive both the employee and the company toward success. If you Google Maslow's theory, you'll see numerous examples of its application to business, including numerous examples and tips on how to fire up employees by understanding their needs. You may see articles pop up on how the theory dovetails with quality management, as applied to organizational dynamics. There are also articles about the psychology of quality management in the context of organizational and business development. That's all fantastic; however, this book is about applying the science of quality management at the most personal level possible with the intended outcome of a 5-star career. If your goal is to build a 5-star worthy career, waiting around for your boss or company to put in such wonderful effort to motivate you is not reliable. Ask yourself this, who is the customer for your company's final product? It's not you. Also, sure, they can seek to understand the common needs of employees, which again, is admirable, but can their initiative tap into your authentic needs, how they evolved, what carrot you may be following, and then determine how best to either move that particular carrot in the direction of their choosing, or take the time to personally move you out a level of need (from Maslow's hierarchy) that you're stuck in? Again, it's good for companies to do these things, but the power *you* hold to do what is needed to grab that big cookie is astronomically higher than theirs. If a company were filled with individuals enjoying, or pursuing 5-star careers, as defined in this book, I believe the potential impact to organizational dynamics and development would be astronomical. Thomas Edison said, "We don't know a millionth of one percent about anything." If we could all focus on better understanding ourselves, which is available to us to do, rather than analyzing other people and groups of people, the world might be a much better place. We might all be eating the big cookie together instead of arguing on Facebook.

If you know that Maslow's ladder exists and that you are secretly driven to climb it, how does that help and what the heck does it have to do with quality management? We'll get there; hang on to your hats (the ones that say Manufacturer and Customer). The rungs on Maslow's ladder represent our basic needs as a card-carrying member of the human species. (Think "birds fly," "fish swim," "babies are cute," and "cows moo.") The bottom rung represents our human needs on a physiological level. If there is no food and water to sustain your life, your need for a job, new running shoes, or a loving mother is not going to take the top spot on your priority list. If you can't live, you'll never get all that other stuff you need anyway. Your best chance is to first find food and water. In fact, Darwin's survival of the fittest theory supports this. Any creature who, for some reason, chose to spend every possible resource available on finding a pair of running shoes, or perhaps inventing them, before finding food and water, did not make it. This likely explains why as a culture, we weren't attuned to "running shoes" until a young guy named Phil Knight visited the Acropolis and was inspired by a feeling that "this is where it all begins." In his memoir, *Shoe Dog*, he tells us that as he stood a few meters from the Temple of Athena Nike, he promised himself that he would someday meet his full potential. If you haven't read *Shoe Dog*, that's your first assignment. Go read it now and come back; don't forget to mark this page.

Although neither Phil Knight, you, nor I were created with anything slightly resembling a cookie cutter we're all driven towards the same giant cookie, *self-actualization*. In Greek civilization, Nike was a goddess who personified victory, which, after all, is the big cookie as well. We need that cookie, and there is nothing wrong with that need, just as there is nothing wrong with a fish needing water. The initial rate at which you were able to move up Maslow's ladder hinged on a complex combination of variables that came at you in a chaotic system over which you had no control, all during a time when your brain was literally forming at incredible speed. Table 7.1 provides examples of who you may expect to find at these levels far into adulthood, including reasons why we sometimes fall back, and why that's okay.

As we enter adulthood and join the workforce, this ladder comes along with us. Your place on this ladder, at any given time, influences your career. Maslow warned of one potential reason why addressing perceived reasons why we don't have what we need is not always easy. He said, "If the only tool you have is a hammer, you tend to see every problem as a nail." Skipping steps on Maslow's ladder is as impossible as skipping months in your

TABLE 7.1

Maslow's Hierarchy of Needs Defined

Ladder Level	Maslow's Phrasing	Focus at Each Level	Types of Adults You Might Find Stuck at Each Level
5	Self-actualization	Desire to become the most that one can be	Adults who do not have unmet needs related to those described in levels 1–4
4	Esteem	Respect, self-esteem, status, recognition, strength, freedom	Adults who do not have unmet needs related to love and belonging, safety, or physiology.
3	Love and belongingness	Friendship, intimacy, family, sense of connection	Adult survivors of childhood abuse, absence or loss of family, dealing with grief – who do not have unmet safety or physiological needs
2	Safety	Personal safety, employment, resources, health, property	Unemployed, chronically ill, in financial trouble, in a physically abusive situation, elderly – who do not have unmet physiological needs
1	Physiological needs	Air, water, food, shelter, sleep, clothing, reproduction	Poverty stricken, mentally ill, struggling with infertility, disabled, elderly

subscription to being alive. Time payments are automatically deducted, and your biological system does not allow movement to the next level of need until the current one has been successfully achieved. It may be that you're stuck at level two, thinking that you're at level three, desperately wanting to get to level four, and you're seeing every issue as a nail. Bang! Bang! Bang! Keep smiling! Bang harder! You got knocked down? So what? Just get up! It's the getting up that matters. Keep banging! And don't forget to think positive. Finally, you yell, "All I have is this hammer! Nobody gave me the toolkit that my colleagues have! It's not fair!"

This is yet another reason why it behooves you to spend some time on additional research and analysis. As a manufacturer, the probability that you can deliver a 5-star career increases with your understanding of the intended customer (you). Manufacturers throughout the world know that making assumptions or skipping this step is not a wise move.

HOW THE SCIENCE OF QUALITY MANAGEMENT FOUND ME STUCK ON MASLOW'S LADDER

I was stuck at level three for many years with a toolkit the size and strength of a Ziplock baggie. As I matured physically and mentally, I became emotionally focused on a golden carrot. I ran toward what I decided was the only possible thing that could validate that I was someone worth loving as a unique individual. As I *tried* to climb the ladder of human needs, my decisions, actions, and plans began to align with moving toward that carrot. Everything else blurred, and by 19, I found myself in an ICU needing a bedpan to catch the activated charcoal forced down my throat the night before. There are times when thinking about the girl in that hospital room overwhelms me. I remember one of her college professors standing outside the large glass ICU room door, no doubt there to visit someone. The girl pulled a thin, woven blanket up around her face to hide. Sometimes I get angry. I wish I could yell through a tunnel of years to tell her what I've learned. I remember her returning to college the following week, telling her friends (who seemed more like acquaintances) that food poisoning was the culprit. She tried to downplay the ordeal, move past it in conversation. She smiled, hearing how they were so glad that she was okay, and went to her next class, and the next, and the next, until 1988 when she left with a degree in biology.

A few years later, I had happily followed my husband from Louisiana to Northern New Jersey to start a new life. Upon arrival, I made a clear decision to leave the girl I'd been behind. I was sure that I could bury her and deal with what had happened to her through writing about it during stolen moments of my days and nights building a career and focusing on being a mother and wife. By the late 1990s, the concepts of identifying customers and collaborators, focusing on processes, and making data-driven decisions were beginning to pop up in the FDA's manufacturing regulations and guidelines due to an increased focus on ensuring that medical devices are safe and effective. Traditionally pharmaceutical manufacturing had been focused on medications rather than machines. Other highly regulated industries such as aerospace and nuclear power were already linked into the science of quality management due to having a solid focus on machinery. Remember, this all started with a focus on the manufacturing of widgets. A machine is essentially a widget that is pieced together in an assembly line; however, a pill is something a bit different. Each piece of a machine has specifications that enable it to dovetail into a product that works as expected. The application of quality management principles was innovative for medical device manufacturing at the time. It didn't take long for the science of quality management to leak into the world of pharmaceutical manufacturing. Industry quality assurance professionals focused on manufacturing were beginning to discuss the topic at industry conferences. It also trickled into corporate-level nonmanufacturing areas that were ready to embrace the idea of improving efficiency and quality as an avenue to save money; this had already occurred in other industries. What *wasn't* such a hot topic was how to apply the science of quality management to nonmanufacturing functions where quality expectations were sky high such as clinical trials, data management, and reporting of adverse events (i.e., side effects of medications). It was difficult for industry professionals to adapt to applying any solutions that were not specifically supported by the FDA. New global guidelines for drug development had made a huge industry splash in the early to mid-1990s and everyone was still digesting and adjusting to those. Considering how to squeeze in the science of quality management was not part of the mindset. Six Sigma outcomes were being widely touted, and many Fortune 100 companies were applying it to special projects and initiatives. To do this, the company required what is referred to as a Six Sigma Black Belt. The *Black Belts* were trained to lead Six Sigma projects, and the training was pricey. To initiate a Six Sigma project or program, the company had to fund Six Sigma training, or hire consultants, and allocate massive amounts of time for various employees to participate.

By this time, I was ten years into my pharmaceutical industry career. I had carved out quality and compliance as a focus and was a manager. When I heard about Six Sigma at an industry conference, I immediately saw the value in applying it to nonmanufacturing functions and their processes, which were my focus at the time. I found out as much as I could and pitched it to the senior management where I worked; I asked them to fund my Six Sigma training so that we could begin to apply the concepts. My request was denied. It was too expensive, and they weren't ready to adopt this crazy thing called Six Sigma. It was a disappointing blow. I couldn't stop thinking about it and questioning why these proven concepts were considered outliers to standard business practice. I wondered what people were taught in business school. As I was going through this thought process, it occurred to me that my company offered tuition reimbursement. They would not pay for a one-week intensive course on quality management, but they were open to funding an entire master's degree. Although that seemed illogical to me, I was thrilled with my new idea. Interestingly, the company that denied my request for Six Sigma training in 1998 now has a global department focused on utilizing the science of quality management to drive process improvements through Six Sigma methodologies and others. I should thank them now. Obtaining a master's degree that encompassed quality assurance and quality systems engineering turned out to be a much better strategy than taking a one-week course on Six Sigma.

A CAREER QUALITY EVENT

My career took off during the time I was working on my graduate degree. I developed and applied a strategy for implementing quality management within my scope as a manager at three different companies, supervising many diverse types of people. It proved to be a successful approach at the mid-management levels in which I was operating. My self-esteem and respect grew! I landed a director-level position at Johnson & Johnson, where I designed and built a new quality-focused function. I finished my degree and wrote *Six Sigma for Business Excellence* (McGraw-Hill). The book relays to middle managers across industries that they don't need a special program or project to implement these concepts; they are simply elements of excellent business practice. I began to view myself as a unique individual. Outside of work, I finished writing my second novel. I'd finally left the strange pain of my childhood behind, determined never to be that person again. Yet, there was an undercurrent of doubt that I couldn't shake. I decided that I could learn to live with that lingering pain. I hoped that if I just pushed through it, year after year, my wound would eventually stop throbbing. What I had was as good as it gets for someone with my story; a 3-star career was quite exceptional; I should be proud of myself and thankful. Then two events beyond my control changed everything.

In 2008, the same year that the US government allocated over $900 billion to special loans and rescues related to the US housing bubble, I experienced what I call a career quality event. Despite my consistent high employee ratings, company awards, a promotion, and other indicators that I was valued, Johnson & Johnson decided to add my name to a lengthy list of employees who would be escorted to the door; I did not see it coming. A major corporate downsizing event was required. It not only surprised me, it cracked the self-identify that I'd worked so hard to create. I felt a snap that day. A crack ran down the sides of who I was, showing me that all I'd done was cover my past with yet another fragile shell. Nothing had been repaired. The protective shell I created as a kid belonged to me. The cracked shell crumbling around me had been an illusion of strength. It was effortlessly broken by a group of strangers required to make a business decision that had nothing to do with me personally. It's tough even now to describe how I felt and how difficult it was to accept. The experience taught me that a career is not a life, and that I'm 100% responsible for both my life and my career. I realized that the strategy and process I'd chosen to build the product I wanted, including my career, had been flawed. I could not cleanly separate the product that is my life from the product that is my career. A 5-star career is part of a 5-star life; a 5-star life is not an outcome of a 5-star career.

I'm thankful that Johnson & Johnson busted my shell that day. It forced me to begin facing my demons. My life started to change in a slow yet productive way that had nothing to do with my job but everything to do with my ability to build my very own 5-star career in the years that followed. Over the next four years, I established myself as a consultant. I continued to gain experience in my field but focused my greatest energy on better understanding my story (the inputs, outputs, processes, mindset, culture, etc.) so that I *could* create a life and a career worthy of 5 stars. For the first time in my life, I made a sincere effort to put aside my pride and be open about my past. I finally accepted that I needed an authentic life. One solid enough to handle hits and events that could potentially impact the quality of the career I was trying so hard to build. I needed a better strategy.

KEY POINTS

1. If most people were simple, we'd be more similar. Sure, we share the human condition, the body, the basic biology, all incredibly important things that connect us, yet drilling down into *exactly* who *you* are, you're alone in your exquisite individuality.

2. The hidden gems of authenticity are found in the intricate assemblage of who you are as an individual. That authenticity is the key to defining what quality means to you.

3. Maslow's widely accepted theory says that consciously or not, as a card-carrying member of the human species, we have a biological need for self-actualization. We carry a deep need to understand and achieve our full potential as unique individuals.

4. The initial rate at which you were able to move up Maslow's ladder hinged on a complex combination of variables that came at you in a chaotic system over which you had no control, all during a time when your brain was forming at incredible speed.

5. If a company were filled with individuals enjoying, or pursuing 5-star careers, as defined in this book, I believe the potential impact on organizational dynamics and development would be astronomical.

6. If we could all focus on better understanding ourselves, which is something available to us to do, rather than analyzing other people and groups of people, the world might be a much better place.

BIBLIOGRAPHY

Abraham Maslow. *Motivation and Personality* (Harper & Brothers, 1954).
Penelope Przekop. *Six Sigma for Business Excellence* (McGraw-Hill, 2005).
Phil Knight. *Shoe Dog: A Memoir by the Creator of Nike* (Scribner, 2018).

8

Manufacturers Build Trust

"All the world is made of faith, and trust, and pixie dust."

—J.M. Barrie, *Peter Pan*

Highly successful companies that achieve longevity have gained the trust of their customers. A seed is planted the first time a customer is satisfied. Then the customer is called upon to have faith that the company can satisfy them again. Trust grows each time the company successfully satisfies the customer, and the level of faith required diminishes. Customer satisfaction is also strengthened or weakened by the company's approach to resolving customer issues. As the seed evolves into a strong, sturdy tree, an occasional dip in satisfaction doesn't make too much of a dent. However, if those dips add up, they can create a giant ax that will bring the trust tree down. Similarly, the severity of *one* dissatisfying outcome can chop down trust as strong as a 300-year-old oak. (In later chapters, I'll circle back to this and explain how you may be able to gain trust in yourself.)

If executed correctly, the science of quality management not only ensures that manufacturers can satisfy their intended customers, it ensures that they can keep them. The aspect of quality customer service provides insight into why service industries began to embrace quality management. Rather than manufacturing tangible widgets, they design and provide customer services. Spend some time on your favorite travel website and you will see this in action. Customer satisfaction lies at the core of how quality is managed, which is why the science has far-reaching applications.

The need to build customer trust also provides insight into why the science has been embraced by industries that develop and deliver products

DOI: 10.4324/9780367855260-8

whose potential flaws can lead to severe outcomes, as well as the global authorities that regulate them. Industries such as aerospace, nuclear power and medicine, and pharmaceuticals evolved to improve the world. However, one crash of an airplane or faulty batch of medication can end lives and trigger far-reaching ripples of emotional and financial devastation. The pioneers of these industries weren't handed roadmaps. Their goal was to build, not destroy, to heal, not to hurt, and this continues to be their goal. That is exactly why these industries not only recognized the science of quality management but also teamed with government agencies around the world to declare its use mandatory. The science is so powerful and successful that it became law for many industries throughout the world.

Just as you can't read this book, wake up tomorrow, and seamlessly apply it to your current system (that may not even be defined) immediately without a hitch, these large global industries continue to move toward a deeper and broader understanding of the science, its associated regulatory requirements, and how to accurately and efficiently apply it. We do that while also striving to meet the needs of our customers and build their trust. The complexity involved in building and retaining customer trust increases with the severity of potential outcomes associated with failure to meet their expectations (i.e., a customer not purchasing the product a second time versus the customer dying).

―――――――

TRUST YOUR MEDS

Not only is quality management front and center during your online shopping, it's also in your hands each time you take your medication. Global regulatory heath authorities require pharmaceutical companies to comply with all applicable laws to ensure patient safety and protect the public. This includes how they manufacture the actual medication as well as how it's tested, how laboratory and clinical data is collected and analyzed, and much more. Regulatory inspectors as well as auditors who work in the industry operate under the premise that if it's not documented, it didn't happen. This is consistent with the burden of proof concept underlying the US legal system and many others around the globe. Pharmaceutical companies develop, document, and implement quality management systems to demonstrate their dedication to ensuring patient safety by adherence to the applicable legal requirements. The documentation involved includes policies and standard operating procedures, protocols, plans, forms, templates, and more. Although the US Congress first passed the Federal Food, Drug, and Cosmetic Act in 1938, the regulations in this area progressed steadily. When I joined the industry in the late 1980s, it was just finding its more comprehensive, modern stride. In 1990, the US Congress passed the Safe Medical Devices Act, which was the first legislation related to medical devices since 1976. The Act modified procedures for the establishment, amendment, or revocation of performance standards, paving the way for dovetailing in the science proven to build quality into widgets. It was a few years later that I heard about Six Sigma and was denied approval to attend a pricey course on this odd-sounding approach to quality. Since that time, led by the European Medicines Agency, regulatory health authorities around the globe increased their focus on the synergies between the regulations they were enforcing across pharma, and the science of quality management.

Today, the science of quality management is used by the industry to *prove* the integrity of clinical data collected and analyzed to *prove* that a new drug is safe and effective. Clinical data integrity and the statistical conclusions of the data analysis are two sides of a coin in the drug development process. Many people only know about the shiny side of that coin (promising results), and therefore lack trust in new vaccines and medications that can prolong and improve quality of life. That two-sided coin is why the pharmaceutical industry has regulatory inspections. Otherwise, the FDA and other global health authorities would simply read a report and provide a yes/no decision. For example, when the FDA reviewed Pfizer, Moderna, and Johnson & Johnson's COVID-19 vaccine clinical trial results, they not only studied the data with a fine-tooth comb, they explored the quality management system in which that data was obtained and analyzed. Just as they require clinical data to be evaluated following proven statistical methods, they require the data to be generated and analyzed within a system that follows the proven science of quality management.

Laws in place throughout the world require both sides of the coin, not just the one most people hear about. Due to this, the pharmaceutical industry is required to not only document our policies and processes, but to also place numerous controls around those critical documents. If a process is going to change, we're required to update the current documented process and document that anyone responsible for executing that process has been trained prior to doing anything different from what the previous documented process reflects. We're even required to have a documented process on how we change an existing documented process. If that's not enough, we're required to generate and retain documentation over the course of drug development (which continues for years) to essentially prove that those responsible were qualified by education, training, and experience for their assigned roles, and that they followed the documented processes.

TRUST REQUIRES INTEGRITY

Ensuring the integrity of customer data in the personal application of the science is paramount and it relies on you. You'll be happy and relieved to know that no one is going to inspect any data or documentation you may happen to develop during or after reading this book. When applied on a personal level, quality is all yours to manage; creating bureaucracy is not the point. Applying quality management to your career development does not require complex documentation; however, integrity is and evaluating oneself objectively can be challenging. We'll focus on how to do that in Chapter 9. The research and analysis conducted to understand your customer (you) require integrity to support the successful delivery of your product, which is a career that has 5-star value to you. I came across several definitions of *integrity*, all similar. Here's the one that popped up on Microsoft Bing:

integrity

NOUN
  1. the quality of being honest and having strong moral principles;
     moral uprightness.
     "he is known to be a man of integrity"
     synonyms:
     honesty · uprightness · probity · rectitude · honor · honorableness
     [more]
  2. the state of being whole and undivided.

"upholding territorial integrity and national sovereignty"
synonyms:
unity · unification · wholeness · coherence · cohesion · undividedness · togetherness · solidarity · coalition
- the condition of being unified, unimpaired, or sound in construction.
  "the structural integrity of the novel"
  synonyms:
  soundness · robustness · strength · sturdiness · solidity · solidness · durability · stability · stoutness · toughness
- internal consistency or lack of corruption in electronic data.
  "integrity checking"

If you're not dedicated to accuracy and integrity in research, you may want to stop reading now. Have you heard someone say, "He's just feeding himself a line of bull?" (Maybe that's a Southern saying; I had a tough time finding it on Google. Regardless, you get the point.) People lie to themselves, often without realizing it, which may be more accurately described as *hiding* rather than *lying*. Blind spots are one way that our subconscious seeks to protect us from uncomfortable, difficult, or painful realities, even when they may have simple solutions. Sometimes, the realities we hide from are easily addressed; doing so can make all the difference. A blind spot may be shielding you from accepting that you're a poor listener, have a negative mindset, or rarely show appreciation for your coworkers. The science of quality management includes the fundamental process of determining root cause and choosing corrective actions that also ensure that the issue does not recur. Exactly how to do this will be covered in more depth, along with examples, in Chapter 13.

With integrity comes truth. I've learned that two things often said about truth are true. It can hurt *and* it can set you free. If you commit to researching your needs and motivations with a fine-tooth comb, and as much integrity as you can muster, the probability of a satisfying outcome will increase dramatically. Be aware that committing to integrity, which also boils down to authenticity, may lead you away from the road you've been traveling. That is the fear that struck me as I sat through the authentic leadership course that required me to share information about my childhood. Although Johnson & Johnson had sent me there, I was afraid that they wouldn't approve of my authenticity. I couldn't muster enough faith to try it just yet. When that fear strikes, faith will be required. Faith in the quality management principles that you have decided to trust, and faith in yourself as the manufacturer. Faith that you can take what you've learned with your customer hat on and use it to manufacture the career that will give you authentic 5-star satisfaction. As you begin to experience those initial sparks of satisfaction, your trust will grow. Eventually, you will believe, and faith will no longer be required.

SOMETIMES FAITH IS REQUIRED

Real change can take quite a while. It wasn't until after I left Johnson & Johnson in 2008 that I slowly began to accept that my approach to overcoming my childhood trauma wasn't working. I was stuck between Maslow's ladder rungs 2 and 3, in a 3-star life and career. Through a blog I created following the publication of my novel, *Aberrations*, I began to publish drips and drabs of my story. I still couldn't verbalize the details; I felt safe writing. (I had explored and shared some of my story in my first two novels with the added buffer of calling it fiction. My novels included details about my life and emotions that I'd never shared with my husband, despite our 17 years together.) I also began painting, sensing that words were not enough to express who I'd been, who I had become, and why. I began the slow road of letting the events of childhood trickle out, despite my fear that it could expose my authenticity and prove I'd somehow managed to land in my current life by being a good fake. It seemed impossible to break out of the mindset I'd developed beginning around 12 years old. Although it felt immature in many ways, I couldn't shake it. Meanwhile, I continued to expand my consulting career, still coasting at 3 stars by my standards.

By 2012, I had made progress in my goal to share more details about my life. I was moving slowly along, determined to focus on the positives in my life. I had come to realize the extent to which I had split myself in half for most of my adult life. I finally wanted to pull it all together; I knew that was the way to free my authenticity, which is what I had desperately wanted my entire life. The two sides of myself were oceans apart.

Then one typical July evening for my family and I in Pennsylvania, my brother, John, walked outside his home on a street called Lost

Lake Lane in Washington state, saluted the American flag hanging on his porch, and shot himself in the head. His 12-year-old daughter was inside playing a video game, headphones in place. (John had installed a camera next to his front door a couple of weeks earlier; the police watched the video of his suicide.) Our phone rang in Pennsylvania and I answered in my usual way, with a smile in my voice. Voices told me that John was dead ... my brother's ex-wife, a police officer, someone else. Their message came at me in a fuzzy language delivered underwater. There was a powerful stop that would never start again, and a start that I knew could not be stopped. The bond John and I shared turned to steel, forged by my attempted suicide at 19 and his death. I felt it as if I were in his body, standing there in his front yard, or maybe sitting, randomly pointing at my Bible, lifting the gun, swallowing the pills, my heavy body dropping as if it no longer obeyed my mind, John falling, maybe a last sad flicker of his eye, looking at me, dead. The girl I so painstakenly hid for almost 20 years exploded. The me that I had shown to the world could not withstand the wave of sorrow that overtook me, bringing with it the strange and painful story that only John and I shared. I wailed. I couldn't stop for months.

By pushing my authentic self away, the one person on the planet who knew his story, I'd taken something authentic from him. I shared that story. I knew what it did to us and how we both tried so hard to be okay. How we both, in our own ways, had chosen to run far away, me to the East Coast, John to the West, and start over. My heart broke every day for months, and I knew that my life had to change. If I failed to own my story, it was always going to own me, hold me back, and steal my power. I couldn't bear for John to die without acknowledgement of that empty space we shared, and I was the only person who *could* acknowledge it. My grief reminded me of how powerless I was a child, and how terrified I had been in a home filled with screaming, demons, and impending disaster.

Pain like that seeks expression; there's a subconscious urge to release the pressure. If you're anything like me, you find a way to feel it. You cut yourself. You put yourself in situations that bring pain. You refuse to be happy. You suffer how you can;. I sobbed over John's death, remembering my own attempted suicide, longing to go back and change it all. Change my life. Change his life. Bring him back. I wanted to be the little girl again who ran next to him in the yard, the girl who sat by him on the school bus, the young adult who looked at him when our mom said something crazy, knowing what the other one knew and felt, even if we couldn't verbalize it. I finally realized how unproductive it was to allow myself that long-suffering type of pain. It's an ongoing release that seems more gentle while squandering the time you have to be happy. It can take a lifetime. It can steal a life. I knew it had to end, and so I sobbed for months over John, over our childhood, over my own regrets and mistakes. I didn't blame myself. I just let myself feel the pain of having a mother who casually informs her child that God is going to kill off their dad. It ushered me into the final phase of accepting the multi-layered terribleness of it all, the deep onion dive that my 12-year-old self took to avoid it, and how all that was happening created a mindset that drove me in circles for years.

PREPARE FOR ACTION

I committed to internalizing what I'd learned about managing quality. I vowed to overcome my fear of disappointing, confusing, or hurting the people I'd spent my life trying to please. That required me to finally trust in my whole self, trust in my good intentions, and trust in what I knew about managing quality. My hope is that the positives in your story far outweigh any negatives, or that at least you've had an average, manageable time of it so far. No one can completely avoid the inherent challenges of the human condition. Every person's story is fascinating, regardless of the height and depth, characters, or curve of the plot. We're a set of bestsellers. Think of all the variations! Sometimes I'm sure that my story is extreme in a strange way, and at other times, I know that it doesn't begin to compare to the stories out there. None of that matters in the context of quality management. It is what it is. It is the "as is" that is waiting to be explored. For each of us, it is the starting point to which we can apply continuous improvements that are applicable, appropriate, to create the product that we want.

You are the expert on you. So, as we dig even farther into the science of quality management, it's imperative that you seek to clear all blind spots, determine where you may be stuck, and find out what carrot may be leading you. I've spent most of my adult life trying to figure all that out, and it was no walk in the park. I'll be honest, the more convoluted and complex the story, the more detail there is to sort through.

The quality of a product must be defined to evaluate it. Further, it must be properly evaluated to identify how it can be improved. In Chapter 9, I'll show you how to do that, and then you'll be ready to accept the challenge following the proven approach used by those who respect and apply the science of quality management.

KEY POINTS

1. A seed is planted the first time a customer is satisfied. Then the customer is called upon to have faith that the company can satisfy them again. Their trust grows each time the company successfully satisfies the customer, and the level of faith required diminishes.

2. If executed correctly, the science of quality management not only ensures that manufacturers can satisfy their intended customer, it ensures that they can keep them.

3. Customer satisfaction lies at the core of every proven application of the science, which is exactly why it has far-reaching applications still waiting to be explored.

4. Pharmaceutical companies develop, document, and implement quality management systems to demonstrate their dedication to ensuring patient safety by adherence to the applicable legal requirements.

5. Clinical data integrity and the statistical conclusions of the data analysis are two sides of a coin in the drug development process. Many people only know about the shiny side of that coin (promising results), and therefore lack trust in new vaccines and medications that can prolong and improve quality of life.

6. Blind spots are one way that our subconscious seeks to protect us from uncomfortable, difficult, or painful realities, even when they may have simple solutions. Sometimes, the realities we hide from are easily addressed; doing so can make all the difference.

7. If you commit to researching your needs and motivations with a fine-tooth comb, and as much integrity as you can muster, the probability of a satisfying outcome will increase dramatically.

8. Every person's story is fascinating, regardless of the height and depth, characters, or curve of the plot. We're a set of bestsellers.

9

Data Is King

"Maybe stories are just data with a soul."

—Brené Brown

Developing a fabulous product is not an overnight activity. No one wakes up one day, saying, "I imagined a product last night, committed to creating it following quality management concepts, did a little research, went to bed, and then woke up to find it, fully formed and 5-star worthy, setting on my bedside table. Woohoo!" Great companies know that trial and error is sometimes necessary to fully understand what may be holding success at bay. The good news is that, most likely, you have already gone through a tremendous amount of trial and error in your career. Now, it's simply a matter of exploring the results of all that data in a new light. This calls for a deeply honest look into your history, attitudes, and blind spots, which is not always easy, but always brings integrity to the exercise.

Applying the science of quality management to career development is an innovative approach backed by over a hundred years of historical proof of concept. If you're open to the challenge, it's time to start manufacturing a 5-star career following the approach used for decades. If you're ready to start, it starts at the top, and you're the leader. My goal as I wrote the last eight chapters was to use what is in my scope of influence to encourage shifts in your existing philosophy and mindset. I'll never know how successful I was; faith is required on my part as we move into the action phase. When industry leaders embrace the science of quality management, officially declaring and sharing their commitment across the company in the form of a quality policy is a powerful first action. Rather than suggest that you put your commitment in writing or even make it now, the best approach in this scenario is to dive into the research and analysis. My theory is that,

DOI: 10.4324/9780367855260-9

based on the highly personal aspects of your product, having your own research to support all that you've read about thus far will go a long way to build your trust in the science. My hope is that you'll emerge at Chapter 10 excited and confident about a commitment to applying the science of quality management to your career. I also recommend this approach because, as I wrote earlier in the book, the written words don't mean anything unless the company and its leader(s) mean them. I don't want you to commit mentally, in writing, or verbally unless you are ready to back it up with action. The actions are what make it real, and what make it work.

With that said, the successful execution of your customer exploration hinges on your willingness to accept the statements below:

- The world at large is an uncontrollable system flying through space and time.
- You have unique talents.
- You are standing at the center of a system that you can identify and control; it is a subsystem in the *world at large*.
- You can choose to conduct the research and analysis required to understand yourself (the customer).
- You can choose to use those results to clarify your product (5-star career).
- You can choose to clearly identify your system and prepare it for the manufacture of that product.
- Going forward, you can monitor your system and product satisfaction, and address issues appropriately to ensure system health and ongoing satisfaction.

This brings us to the dovetailing third and fourth concepts introduced in Chapter 1:

1. Life is not a process nor is your career. Your career is a *product* created by your process.
2. Quality is defined by the customer; the quality of your products (career/life) is defined by you.
3. **Quality cannot be accurately rated or improved until it's defined.**
4. **You are 100% responsible for your product.**

MEET YOUR CUSTOMER TO DEFINE *QUALITY*

At this point, you may be scratching your head, wondering how the heck are you going to research and analyze your customer (you). Depending on how introspective you are, you may have been mulling over your story for years, or you may have been meeting with your therapist for years. What else can you possibly do? Well, you can put on your manufacturing hat and choose to view your story from the quality management perspective used in industry to determine root causes of customer motivations, quality events, and decisions that led to the situations at play. If you're naturally less introspective, I urge you to embrace these concepts and try it. As I'm sure you may have heard, nothing changes if nothing changes. In industry, the manufacturer is 100% responsible for their product. The buck always stops there. Outsourcing within the pharma industry serves as a fitting example. Global regulatory agencies, such as the US FDA, hold the pharma company responsible for adhering to all applicable regulations for the products they develop and market, regardless of outsourcing. This means that a pharma company can pay another company to manage a clinical trial (e.g., a vendor); however, the pharma company is responsible for oversight of the company to which they delegated responsibility. The pharma company must have documented evidence of their vendor oversight. If something goes terribly wrong during a clinical trial, by law, it is unacceptable for the pharma company to point a finger at the vendor and say, "They did it." Another example is that a parent cannot leave a two-year-old at home all day, and then says, "It was my two-year-old's fault," when something goes wrong. Finally, when their 1-star-rated product doesn't meet sales goals, a manufacturer who points a finger at customers, saying, "It's their fault; they have no idea what they want or need," is simply wrong. When following the science of quality management, you are 100% responsible for the quality of your product, which is incredibly powerful and positive. In that case, it behooves you to research and analyze your story from the new perspective. At the end of this chapter, I'll ask you to do just that and provide you with tools to do it.

During the 1990s, nobody at the large pharma companies I worked for focused on self-reflection, unless it was somehow related to your next career move; all other self-reflection was personal and considered unrelated to and a distraction to the work. In fact, work/life balance didn't exist as a topic in the pharma industry; it may have even seemed like a dirty word at the time, something that meant you lacked dedication. In 1993, I was part of a laboratory research team for a large pharma company; our focus was dermatology. The various teams were gearing up for the annual off-site departmental event. It would be fun and informative. Each team would present on the research we'd conducted over the last year. In addition to our team presentations, three coworkers and I decided to bravely present data and information related to working mothers. This was a huge deal for us. We were incredibly nervous about how it would be perceived, and if there might be negative ramifications for us. In the end, I'm not sure how much of an impact we made; however, we felt, and I still feel, that we played a small role in moving the needle of work/life balance towards where it sits today.

Times have changed. Last year, while working with a biotech company based in California, I attended a company-wide virtual meeting in which the first ten minutes was reserved for quiet self-reflection. A woman with a soothing voice suggested topics, emotions, etc., that we could potentially reflect on, which primarily consisted of all things human rather that all things *work*. I got the feeling that anyone who was not interested in taking the time for this may be viewed as backward, a robotic business puppet or puppeteer. I closed my eyes and reflected, thinking about those three co-workers of mine, and how stressed we were about our poster. We were innovative thinkers in 1993, yet now I wondered if I was getting "old" in the workplace, considering this was the first time I'd participated in a self-reflection activity during this sort of business meeting. It seemed like a perfectly normal agenda item to everyone else on the call. Although I wasn't sure if that level of self-reflection at work was necessary; it was fascinating, and I've thought a lot about it. I certainly don't believe that anyone who skips self-reflection alone or during a meeting is backward in any way. The shift toward work/life balance in the workplace has been a fantastic one. Companies are more open than ever to reinventing the way we work, the way we think about work, and to exploring innovative approaches for how we can create more integrated lives. In 2020, Covid-19 accelerated that shift on a global scale.

DATA IS KING

The science of quality management includes data-driven decision making and management. Data is king, which is one of the reasons why the science of quality management falls into the STEM bucket. In Chapter 2, you read how the science took root on the widget manufacturing floor. Over the 100 years that followed, it grew and meandered its way into industry after industry, across the globe, then hooked up with technology, and wove into global laws that ensure public safety. Today it meets your gaze each time you rate products and services online, take your mediations, and buckle up on a flight. The data focus has been on using objective data to make decisions and manage processes, and on using subjective data as it relates to understanding customers and their satisfaction.

Objective data is factual and provides accurate indisputable conclusions. An objective statement is based on facts. It can be easily proven and is impossible to deny. Therefore, more university math and statistics courses are required by the engineering department than by the psychology department. Research in the psychology field is much more subjective.

Subjective research focuses on experiences from the perspective of an individual and emphasizes the importance of personal viewpoints and interpretations. It comes to play when exploring customer satisfaction with finished products or services, for example, when a customer is asked to rate their level of satisfaction (which is subjective) with a hotel stay. This type of data is most often associated with emotions. In experimental psychology and medical science, a subjective report is information collected from an experimental subject's description of their own experiences, symptoms, or histories. Subjective reporting is the act of an individual describing their own subjective experience, following their introspection on physical or psychological effects under consideration. The method of subjective report analysis also encompasses obtaining information from a subject's own recollection, such as verbal case histories, or experiences in the individual's wider daily life.

During the communication process, you're called upon to separate the two types of data and use it to form conclusions. This happens both subconsciously and consciously as you interpret information communicated to you in relation to everything else happening around you. Our ability to do this strengthens as we grow up. Small children typically lack a sophisticated ability to differentiate between objective and subjective information, and are reliant on adults to help them navigate, learn, and grow. During and following puberty, teenagers often struggle on a different level as they find themselves in new situations, needing to assess more complex information, all while being bombarded by hormones. Once we reach adulthood, we've developed a sophisticated ability to digest data and information. Unfortunately, there are a cornucopia of reasons why many adults continue to confuse subjective and objective data and information, even when having to deal with the consequences that may result. Additionally, when people understand the difference, they may nevertheless struggle with decision making, due to the emotions involved. Confusing objective and subjective data and information can have negative, even disastrous effects, on both the confused individual, and those around them. The story below provides an example.

WHAT COLOR IS THE SKY?

Several years ago, I created a painting titled "All Alone in a World with a Green Sky." It was my visual attempt to express emotions involved when someone in your life confuses objective truth with subjective opinion on a major scale. The painting's central figure is a distraught woman sitting alone next to a body of water beneath a green sky. She is holding her knees to chest and is naked. She looks as if she just can't take it anymore. A rowboat is in the water, as if waiting to take her somewhere. She knows that the sky is (generally) blue. She also knows what blue looks like. These are objective facts. However, she's dealing with someone who insists that the sky is (generally) green, as if it were an objective fact. It was my mother who told me that the sky is green. The sky is a metaphor for all the things she told me were facts before I understood the facts. There is a reason why she sees a green sky and remains convinced that the rest of us are wrong. Imagine you're a small child beneath a giant blue sky being told that it's green by the most important person in your life. You look up and register the information as an objective fact; you assume the color you see is green. You have no idea that the adult holding your hand is looking through a lens that you don't need. In school, people show you blue, and you think it's green. You're puzzled and ask your mother about this. She confirms that it's green. It doesn't make sense, but you trust her, feeling guilty for your doubt. When reasonable people tell you that your mother is wrong, you defend her. As you grow up, people continue to tell you that sky is blue, not green, looking at you as if you're crazy, flawed, or somehow broken. They can't understand why someone as smart as you can't seem to grasp that the sky is blue; it's so simple! A part of you, if not all, is lonely and confused. Finally, as an adult you learn to accept that the sky is and always was blue. It's beautiful! It becomes easier and easier to truly see that giant sky, and so you are struck by all the unnecessary difficulty you endured. You realize that you weren't allowed to decide for yourself what color the sky was, and so you must work through the process of shifting your mindset, accepting that green doesn't look like blue, that your mother was wrong, and that you fell for it. You work through wondering what else your mother was and is wrong about, knowing that it's much more than the color of the sky. You work to forgive yourself for being so gullible and needy. You remind yourself that you had no other frame of reference; you were a small child whose brain was developing. You move forward, struggling to trust what others tell you, and to believe in your own thoughts, opinions, and reality. And all the while, your mother continues to call every day to remind you that the sky is green. You do the best you can to remember that the sky is blue, that it's there as you look out of your office window every day, and that you'll never be able to change your mother's mind. Once you realize that it's not and never has been within your scope to make her see the sky as blue, you'll be free to step into that boat and sail away to wherever it is you choose to go.

THE DANGER OF ILLOGICAL LEAPS

The story above adds a visual aspect that may help you understand and remember how objective and subjective data differ, and why it's an important distinction. You can't deny objective data; it essentially does not belong to you. However, your subjective data and information belong to you. You can choose to keep it as is or change it. You can make a case as to why someone may want to consider changing their subjective data, but no one can or should make that change other than that person. Juries are provided facts and other supporting evidence on which to base a decision; then they are left to make that decision. The law is structured this way because it intends to produce a quality decision. A couple of years ago, I was foreman of a jury that deliberated a medical malpractice case for four days. The experience provided me absolute certainty that in a room of individuals, the ability to differentiate objective and subjective data and information and apply it to decision making that will result in quality is wildly inconsistent. There were jurors who had an unbelievable struggle with applying objective evidence to their thought process due to either their emotions about what happened to the patient, or due to hyper-focusing on one aspect of the situation that, on its own, did not support a logical conclusion. If you've never seen the timeless 1957 film, *12 Angry Men*, I highly commend grabbing some popcorn and spending the time to watch it.

To help solidify how the distinction between objective and subjective data can drive our interactions and decisions, consider the following scenarios:

- If you think red is the best color there is, you're free to change your mind tomorrow, and go with yellow; this is subjective. It would be illogical to *expect* your friend, Pete, to agree that yellow is the best color. It would also be illogical to conclude that Pete is not too sharp when he disagrees; he thinks that blue is the best color. Pete can decide blue is the best color. It has no bearing on your choice. It's acceptable for you to share with Pete what you love about yellow. After he listens, he can choose to agree and switch to yellow, or stay with blue.

- On the other hand, imagine that during a hiking trip, Pete finds a ridge above a lake and is thinking about jumping. You happen to know that the water below is only 3 feet deep although from where Pete stands it may appear to be much deeper. You provide this objective data (the water is 3 feet deep) so that he doesn't jump. Pete can spend a lifetime trying to convince you (or anyone else) that the lake is 20 feet deep but he will be wrong. The depth of the lake is irrefutable. Concerned for his safety, you're justified in doing whatever possible to stop him from jumping. If he chooses to reject the objective information provided, and jumps off the ridge, you will need to call 911. Pete made an illogical leap; it was his decision to make it. He will suffer the consequences. If he recovers only to blame you; that is also illogical. It was not your decision nor was the outcome your fault. If you purposely withheld the information and said, "Go ahead, jump!" you bear a huge responsibility in his decision. If he jumps before you have a chance to warn him, it's not your fault.

It's your right and responsibility to evaluate information that comes your way. Accepting this and seeking to do so following the approach proven to produce a 5-star quality product is critical to researching and analyzing your story. It also drives decision making within a quality system. Unfortunately, many people lack a clear understanding of the distinction between objective and subjective data, and how that categorization logically applies to communication, perception, problem solving, decision making, and continuous improvement. Learning this as I studied and applied quality management concepts during my career led me to a life-changing paradigm shift.

PUT ON YOUR MANUFACTURING HAT

There is objective and subjective data in your story. Understanding the distinction between them is a game changer when mining your unique story. It's possible to identify, compile, and process data of both types to gain insight on how and why your current job/career isn't 5-star worthy, and how you can continuously improve by applying the science of quality management going forward. Looking at your data from a quality management perspective can dramatically improve your decision-making process as well as your level of satisfaction with those decisions. Data-supported decisions will keep you on the right path. At the end of this chapter, I'll recommend that you set this book aside, put on your manufacturing hat, and explore your own story to identify data that can tell you more about your customer (you). To do this, I've designed a unique downloadable Story Data Mining Tool that's available (at no charge) on my website: www.penelopeprzekop.com. During the exercise, you may catch yourself confusing the two types of data at times. If so, pause to clarify which type of information it is, and how the information contributed to subsequent events. Both types of data are important! Table 9.1 provides example questions, and high-level answers and analysis from my story.

TABLE 9.1

Example of Story Data Mining Exercise

Childhood Example Questions

Story Question 1 — **Did you grow up in one geographic area (for the most part)?**

Answer — Yes

Is this an objective or subjective answer? — Objective

Analysis — This question asks for an objective answer. The answer provided is objective.

Story Question 2 — **How many homes did you live in by the time you were 18 years old?**

Answer — 4

Is this an objective or subjective answer? — Objective

Analysis — This question asks for an objective answer. The answer provided is objective.

Story Question 3 — **What geographic culture did you grow up in (for the most part)?**

Answer — It was a culture filled with people who were kind, but I didn't trust them.

Is this an objective or subjective answer? — Subjective

Analysis — This question asks for an objective answer such as the *Bible Belt* or the *Southern US*. The answer is subjective. It is an opinion about the people who lived where I grew up, and my feelings about them. I should consider why I didn't trust people. Why did I feel compelled to say this when it wasn't the question that was asked of me?

Story Question 4 — **How did you feel about the culture you grew up in?**

Answer — It was a culture filled with people who were kind, but I didn't trust them. We went to church three times a week.

Is this an objective or subjective answer? — Subjective

(Continued)

TABLE 9.1 (CONTINUED))

Example of Story Data Mining Exercise

Analysis	This question asks for a subjective answer. The answer provided is subjective. When considered with the objective answer of the Bible Belt for Question 3, this presents a conflict. Theoretically, those who follow the Bible should be trustworthy. Why the distrust? *Note:* we went to church three times a week is an *objective* statement that doesn't directly answer the question.

Work History Example Questions

Story Question 1

Were you ever fired from a job?	
Answer	Yes
Is this an objective or subjective answer?	Objective
Analysis	This question asks for an objective answer. The answer provided is objective.

Story Question 2

Why were you fired, according to your employer?	
Answer	They said that I was talking to another employee too much. Although true, it was not my fault. I was 17. The other employee was a creepy guy who would not leave me alone. I tried to avoid him, but he would not stop bothering me when I was working. I didn't want to hurt his feelings or seem unkind.
Is this an objective or subjective answer?	Subjective although the questions asked for an objective answer.
Analysis	This question asks for an objective answer, which is provided at first but then downplayed by a subjective explanation to explain that it was not my fault, which can also be interpreted as "I had no power to keep my job; it was out of my hands." What could I have done to avoid getting fired? Here are a few choices that were available to me (and would have been acceptable for a 17-year-old to take):
	• Clearly and directly ask my co-worker to stop talking to me rather than trying to passively avoid him.

(Continued)

TABLE 9.1 (CONTINUED))

Example of Story Data Mining Exercise

	• Tell my employer that my co-worker is not picking up on my obvious hints that I'm busy, and that I'm not sure what do. Tell the employer that I want to do an excellent job and am uncomfortable about confronting my co-worker more directly.
	• Ask my employer to move me to another area.
	Why didn't I take any of those actions? I didn't want to hurt my co-worker's feelings. I was avoiding conflict. I wanted to be a nice person. I wasn't skilled at being direct.
	Why was that so important to me? I grew up in the Bible Belt.
	Who did I give my power to? My co-worker.
	Was he the customer for my 5-star job/career? Absolutely not.
	In this scenario, I had a quality event and chose an incorrect action to address it. (We'll focus on quality events later in the book). My answer demonstrated that at the time, I did not accept 100% responsibility for my product (job), nor did I understand that I was the customer of my product (what I wanted – to have a job where I felt comfortable).
Story Question 3	**If fired, do you recall thinking that you learned anything from it at the time, and if so, what did you think you learned?**
Answer	I learned that I did not want to work at a department store, and to be careful about who I was friendly to at work.
Is this an objective or subjective answer?	Subjective
Analysis	If I had known or learned the concept noted in the Story Question 2 analysis, the experience would have made a much greater impact on my work/career going forward. I see now that I didn't learn anything of true value from it at all. I already knew that I didn't want to work in a department store long term. I can think of other work/career situations following that job when I gave my power away to others as well. This issue slowed down my progress, and/or kept me from being satisfied with my work for quite some time.

(Continued)

TABLE 9.1 (CONTINUED))

Example of Story Data Mining Exercise

Story Question 4	What were the toughest things for you to adjust to in your first job after finishing your education, and do they still bother you now?
Answer	One of those things was that I didn't like working nine to five. I loved the flexible schedule of college as compared to high school so when I was back to a consistent schedule, I felt trapped. I never missed class in college but in high school and in my first job, I stayed home sick a lot, which I knew was not good. Yes, it has bothered me for my entire career. Now I'm a consultant, which I love. Part of why I love it is that I have a flexible schedule.
Is this an objective or subjective answer?	Subjective
Analysis	Now I realize that instead of putting myself down for not wanting to go to work five days a week on a nine to five schedule, I could have identified this as an important specification for me, and that there's nothing wrong with that. Ergo, I could use that knowledge to make career decisions that would lead me towards my 5-star career. (With that said, sometimes you must do what you must do, even if you don't love it. However, you can use the knowledge to create and adjust your plans and goals earlier in your career. You can give yourself a break and save time and stress by accepting that it's okay if working a consistent schedule prescribed by others does not enable you to be as authentic as possible. Now you know something that is important to you at an authentic level.)

Note: answer the questions from the perspective you had at the time, which may or may not be your current perspective. Try to recall what you were thinking and feeling at that time. This will enable you to reflect on the philosophy, mindset, priorities, decision making, etc., that were in play at that time.

The example is a simplified version of what you will find in the downloadable Story Data Mining Tool. The tool includes both objective and subjective questions. It's an Excel file that also includes detailed instructions that you won't find here. The example used in Table 9.1 is intended to relay some of the basic concepts involved in the exercise.

I have no choice but to defer to you to make the decision to spend the time required to complete the Story Data Mining Tool. I highly recommended doing so and hope that you will! Some readers may feel satisfied with reading through the examples above and considering how the thought process might apply to them. Others may want to dig into the downloadable questions and use the tool to reflect on how their unique story has informed their adult life and career. It's an exploratory exercise designed to assist you in taking an objective look at your story to identify current processes, carrots, lessons learned, lessons missed, how you process objective and subjective information, and how all of that has informed your decisions, etc. This is needed to identify gaps, make process improvements, and continue forward. My approach supports the premise that you are the manufacturer of your career and the extent to which you choose to consider how your past has informed the present, and can inform the future, is your choice just like everything else. If you choose not to download, that's fine.

Keep in mind that the Story Data Mining Tool is only helpful if you are committed to integrity in your research. If you put garbage into an equation, you'll get a garbage answer. That's how it works. Neither I, nor anyone else, will ever know how honest your answers and thought process will be as you complete the tool, or read this book. It takes courage to be honest with oneself; however, there is no risk associated with doing so in this scenario. The risk lies in dishonesty. Growth requires honesty; without it, you risk being in a more-of-the-same manufacturing scenario. A product cannot be improved if customer information is inaccurate, skewed, or false. As a manufacturer of your 5-star career, failing to have accurate customer information will cause you to miss the point and waste time, money, and energy. If you can't be honest with yourself in a situation where no one else is involved, you will likely get to the end of this book and continue in your life as is. Completing the exercise may call upon you to reflect on experiences, facts, and/or past decisions that cause a sting you prefer to avoid. However, if you want to see something different happen in your life and career, that sting may be required. Like getting a shot, it's best to accept that it will hurt but that it's a necessary pain considering the benefit it offers. As with any type of pain, some of us feel it more than others. We're all unique, but we can all survive the sting.

This is the moment when I encourage you to set aside this book and spend some time with the Story Data Mining Tool available as a free download on my website: www.penelopeprzekop.com. The Excel spreadsheet includes detailed instructions and thought-provoking analysis questions to support the activity. Remember these important points (all of these and much more will be in the tool for you as well):

- No one else is going to read or analyze the information you add to the tool. It's for you. You'll receive the most benefit by allowing yourself to be as honest as possible in both your answers and analysis.
- For each question, do your best to answer based on who and where you were at the time, considering both your age and mindset.
- During the analysis, keep in mind the four concepts shared below. Consider whether your answers reflect the concepts in any way. If not, what concepts were you operating under at the time? As a reminder, here they are again:

1. Life is not a process nor is your career. Your career is a *product* created by your process.
2. Quality is defined by the customer; the quality of your product (career/life) is defined by you.
3. Quality cannot be accurately rated or improved until it's defined.
4. You are 100% responsible for your product.

It's difficult, if not impossible, to achieve a 5-star career using the science of quality management unless you're willing and able to truly own your story and accept it as a rich repository of data that can identify your "as-is" process. It doesn't matter if you view your story as exciting, boring, tragic, sad, short, too long, or like a walk in a rose garden. The goal is to gain insight on what may be holding you back from operating in a system that drives your personal definition of success. Owning your story is the first step toward creating a path forward using quality management concepts and methodologies.

(For those who plan to tackle the recommended assignment now, good luck. Be sure to put this book somewhere you'll remember. I'll be waiting for you in Chapter 10.)

KEY POINTS

1. Based on the highly personal aspects of your product, having your own research to support all that you've read about thus far will go a long way to build your trust in the science.
2. When following the science of quality management, you are 100% responsible for the quality of your product, which is incredibly powerful and positive. In that case, it behooves you to research and analyze your story from the new perspective.
3. The shift toward work/life balance in the workplace has been a fantastic one. Companies are more open than ever to reinventing the way we work and to exploring innovative approaches for how we can create more integrated lives.
4. The science of quality management includes data-driven decision making and management. Data is king, which is one of the reasons why the science falls into the STEM bucket.
5. Objective data is factual and provides accurate indisputable conclusions. An objective statement is based on facts. It can be easily proven and is impossible to deny.
6. Subjective research focuses on experiences from the perspective of an individual and emphasizes the importance of personal perspectives and interpretations. It comes to play when exploring customer satisfaction with finished products or services, for example, when a customer is asked to rate their level of satisfaction (which is subjective) with a hotel stay. This type of data is most often associated with emotions.

7. It's your right and responsibility to evaluate information that comes your way. Accepting this and seeking to do so following the approach proven to produce a 5-star quality product is critical to researching and analyzing your story. It also drives decision making within a quality system.

8. If you put garbage into an equation, you'll get a garbage answer.

BIBLIOGRAPHY

Alan Richardson, Subjective Experience: Its Conceptual Status, Method of Investigation, and Psychological Significance. *The Journal of Psychology: Interdisciplinary and Applied* 133(5), 469–485 (1999). doi:10.1080/00223989909599756

10

Strategize for Quality

"Strategy is a style of thinking, a deliberate process, an intensive implementation system, the science of ensuring future success."

—Pete Johnson, American boogie-woogie and jazz pianist

Welcome back!

The time has come to pull all the information you've gleaned from both this book and your story together and start manufacturing what you want. Using the best approach possible given that I don't know you or the specifics of your story and career to date, I'll explain how to apply the science of quality management to your career. I'm relying on you to insert your personal details and thought process into the exercise. I'm comfortable with this because I know that the science of quality management can be applied to any product, including a career.

As we go forward, you should know that data is frequently imperfect and incomplete, This could be the case with your story data or the extent to which you're confident in your analysis. If so, that's okay! The exercise had several purposes:

1. To enhance your understanding of objective versus subjective data and information, and perhaps identify any tendencies you may have toward a more objective or subjective thought process. If so, you may have seen that this impacted your decision-making process.
2. To inspire you to consider where you may be on Maslow's hierarchy of needs, and if this has impacted your behaviors and decisions, and how.

DOI: 10.4324/9780367855260-10

3. To consider what your philosophies and mindset were at various times during your career and how that may have impacted decisions and outcomes.

4. To consider how you perceived and approached career quality events, including your thought process. Perhaps it was more focused on blaming or depending on people or situations outside the scope of your influence, or perhaps you see now that you didn't use the resources available to you in those cases.

5. To give you practice on evaluating past behaviors, beliefs, and decisions so that you can compare, and contrast them with what I'm going to share with you now.

To obtain the best possible value from this book, I ask that you keep the five items above in mind as we go forward. I must rely on you to use the type of insight described above to compare your story and analysis with the approach that will be described going forward. That's how you can begin to clarify, for yourself, how you can shift or improve what you've done in the past and create a 5-star career manufacturing process. Although it may seem disruptive, I'm going to remind you to do this every now and then throughout the rest of the book. It's important!

You should not let a concern about incomplete or imperfect data paralyze your career or push it in the direction of flying blind. Move forward with the data you have. Then you can strive to improve your story data quality and completeness over time but be aware of the diminishing returns in your quest for data perfection. None of us will ever have access to all the variables at play in our story; therefore, it is fruitless to believe that we can arrive at perfection in our understanding or analysis. This is another reason why it behooves us to place focus on ourselves, our responsibilities, and the variables that fall within the scope of our influence. During your story data analysis, you may also have encountered unexpected insights that seem unrelated to the questions and answers you were analyzing. Exploration and discovery are why many of us enjoy performing analysis. You never know what you'll learn about yourself, and/or the process you've followed.

Regardless of the depth and breadth of your story-related thoughts, this is when you move forward, draw a line in the sand, and start the first day of the rest of your life. You get to decide what to bring with you, and what to leave behind. As I mentioned earlier, the purpose of this book is not to relay a cookie cutter solution. I can't do that due to how incredibly unique you are. My goal is to encourage you to approach the manufacture of your career, and possibly your life, in a new way. How new that will be is up to you. Your life may be working well in multiple ways that you're happy about. Only you know this. You're the customer for your product, and you are also the manufacturer who is 100% responsible for its quality. That makes you the only individual on the planet who can determine how the science of quality management will be most useful. Imagine the power manufacturers have when they are also customers of their product. I'm sure you've heard stories of people who have developed amazing products due to their own need for it. I tend to put a lot of initial trust in those types of products, knowing that it was created by someone who specifically needed the same thing I need. You have that level of power over the trajectory and outcome of your life and career. When this realization finally reached the depth required for me, given my personal story, it was mind-blowing.

THE STRATEGY PROVEN TO WORK

The first step toward successfully applying the science of quality management to your career is to make the decision to follow the proven strategy you've been reading about. You read about quality management strategy earlier, particularly from the perspective of industry leaders who set out to lead their organizations in following the science of quality management. Now, let's consider personal strategy. This is a concept that I struggled with as a young adult; it confused me due to some other dovetailing information being thrown my way such as networking, collaborating, planning, creating processes, etc. I used to think, "How the heck is having a plan different from having a strategy?"

Like many employees, I wasn't instructed or encouraged to think strategically until reaching a particular level in my career. For me, the word *strategy* began popping up in relation to my work when I became a senior manager. I had been in the workforce, same industry, for about 13 years. Once you work your way to a position in which the word *strategy* starts to fly, you may have a feeling that you're supposed to know how to make the shift from tactical to strategic thinking. You may be wondering why a person wouldn't simply ask their boss: "What is strategy?" That's a good question, and there are assorted reasons why someone would not ask, several of which may be related to Maslow's ladder. Let's face it, sometimes we get into the odd situations that cause these blips. What if you were just hired for your new job, which is a promotion, because somehow based on what you've done and how you communicated, your new boss felt confident that you could strategize. Okay, maybe you can, but you're still wondering how that differs from planning. Meanwhile, most of us primarily operate tactically outside the workplace. We have long lists of personal responsibilities that require rolling up sleeves and getting stuff done. If you're a naturally strategic thinker, that's a plus. However, without a solid framework for a brain that's constantly trying to connect the dots, your strategies can veer out of control and land way off the mark. (I know this firsthand.) Have you ever had anyone at work say something like this to you, "You're describing a plan. What's your strategy?" looking at you as if you're less than because you're still planning rather than strategizing? If so, you may have found yourself scratching your head, stressed about what your answer should be.

Well, guess what, *strategy* is defined as a plan of action or policy designed to achieve a major or overall aim. Other definitions include:

- An action that managers take to attain one or more of the organization goals
- A careful plan or method

Strategy is a synonym for *plan*. So, whether you refer to it as a strategy or a plan is irrelevant. It's grammatically awkward to refer to someone as a *planning thinker*; however, the strange sounding phrase actually describes *strategic thinking*. It is thinking about what is happening now in the context of a plan or thinking of a plan within the context of what is happening now. The science of quality management calls for creating a plan *and* thinking strategically as you execute that plan. Why? Because sometimes plans don't go as smoothly as you imagined. I'll focus specifically on that reality in Chapter 13.

If you're thinking that your actual job today isn't strategic, think again. McDonald's is *McDonald's* because two guys realized that developing a strategy (i.e., plan) for making a fresh burger and quickly handing it to a customer through a window would improve their business. Whether you're a teacher, attorney, store manager, or hair stylist, applying strategic thinking to the work that you do and products you contribute to is one of the most valuable skills you can offer. As you learn to think strategically within the context of quality management to build a 5-star career, you'll also begin to develop and deliver high-quality work-specific deliverables that benefit your boss, direct reports, customers, leadership, and company. Implementing quality management concepts will allow you to demonstrate strategic thinking. Considering the wide variety of career scenarios out there and the complexity and uniqueness we each possess, there are probably numerous strategies encompassing the underlying concepts of quality management that could be applied. As we've established, my goal is not to hand you a cookie cutter solution. My goal is to provoke thought and provide information, examples, and ideas that can get you started on a quality management path, which is highly individual. In this book, the focus is on developing a career that brings you the highest possible level of intrinsic satisfaction; however, I hope that you will also consider how the concepts can be applied specifically to your daily work. That is icing on the cake for you! A double whammy that will likely speed up production of your 5-star career.

Industry leaders who understand and embrace the philosophy and mindset fundamental to the science of quality management act to execute a proven strategy. In Figure 3.1, you saw an illustration of how the various components discussed in Chapter 3 connect to create that high-level strategy. Similarly, Figure 10.1 illustrates how the same components can create the same powerful domino effect to support the manufacture of your 5-star career.

Many of us settle into a focus on the philosophy or mindset steps in Figure 10.1 when trying to improve areas of our life, including career. We believe that if we possess or continue to develop a fantastic philosophy, mindset, or attitude, we will eventually succeed. All these things and more may work for some; they are wonderfully powerful ideas that drive forward movement. However, based on the science of quality management, as well as my professional knowledge and experience of how best to build and manage quality, none of these components alone are enough. Sometimes, we do our best to forge ahead only to find our career lacking by our own personal standards, or even failing to get started. This can be both discouraging and confusing. We can fall into the trap of blaming ourselves and others for all the things that held us back or continue to do so. (Reminder: don't forget to process this in relation to your story

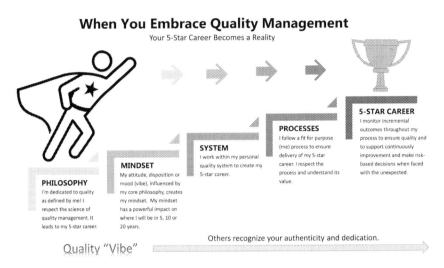

When You Embrace Quality Management
Your 5-Star Career Becomes a Reality

5-STAR CAREER
I monitor incremental outcomes throughout my process to ensure quality and to support continuously improvement and make risk-based decisions when faced with the unexpected.

PROCESSES
I follow a fit for purpose (me) process to ensure delivery of my 5-star career. I respect the process and understand its value.

SYSTEM
I work within my personal quality system to create my 5-star career.

MINDSET
My attitude, disposition or mood (vibe), influenced by my core philosophy, creates my mindset. My mindset has a powerful impact on where I will be in 5, 10 or 20 years.

PHILOSOPHY
I'm dedicated to quality as defined by me! I respect the science of quality management. It leads to my 5-star career.

Others recognize your authenticity and dedication.

Quality "Vibe"

FIGURE 10.1
When you embrace quality management: your 5-star career becomes a reality.

data and analysis.) Earlier in the book, I mentioned quite a few experts who have provided fantastic advice and mind-blowing insight supported by the scientific study of psychology. I spent time making the point that you can be motivated out the wazoo by all that power-packed advice yet somehow lack the basic engine needed to turn all that positive advice into the outcomes you desire. The science of quality management needs a seat at that table. I suggest that quality management is the table, and that if all those psychological concepts and philosophical ideas could pull their chair up closer, many of us may gain a heck of a lot more clarity. There's a place for all of it. However, many people run into a perplexing gap when they set out to apply all those ideas scattered around the bookcase. Understanding how quality is defined, built, and managed was the missing link for me.

In Chapter 11, I'll focus on defining your scope of influence (i.e., your system), and sharing the high-level process you can use to operate within that system to drive results.

IS PERSONAL STRATEGY OPPORTUNISTIC?

The terms *plan* and *strategy* can have different connotations. While *strategy* is more often associated with war, James Bond, corporate intrigue, and political debates, *plan* tends to be associated with family vacations, teaching curricula, what's for dinner, and what you want to be when you grow up. After progressing to director level in my career, I began to hear *think strategically* every day, sometimes multiple times a day. I still struggled with how to implement this, along with the idea of networking. Based on the culture I grew up in, the connotative aspects, my family history, and my genetic disposition, both strategy and "proactively interacting with others to make beneficial connections" (which is how it was described at the time) seemed a tad self-serving with a sprinkle of slime. Meanwhile, I was a person who had used creative thinking my entire life either to ensure that my needs were met as a kid, or as an adult, to determine how to navigate a world where most of those around me knew the sky was blue long before I did. So, when a boss of mine, who I admired, casually described me as opportunistic during that time in my life, I was deeply disturbed. When applied to people, the label "opportunist" also tends to carry a negative connotation. It implies that the person takes unprincipled, unfair advantage of opportunities for selfish ends. Opportunistic people are often regarded as exploitative.

While I'm far from perfect, I'm not, nor have I ever been, one to take unprincipled, unfair advantage of others for my own gain. My boss was brilliant; I assumed she knew what *opportunistic* implied. Choosing to use the term to describe me was not only upsetting, it was puzzling. I felt horrible about it until I realized that being opportunistic, *when well-intended*, is another way to describe someone with a knack for noticing and connecting dots, understanding where they might lead, and making decisions to either continue in a current direction, or change course. A person who understands the goal, and then proactively looks for dots that can connect in creative ways to create a path that leads to success is a *planning thinker*. A person who can recognize opportunities and use them in positive ways, or who has natural strategic thinking skills may certainly use them for their own selfish ends. Just as someone with natural leadership skills can grow up to lead a crime ring or a successful corporation that creates positive change in the world. Once I realized that *opportunistic* is sort of like *strategic* spelled backwards, my perspective began to change, especially in terms of how I viewed myself. Although I'm still not sure that she chose quite the right word, doing so triggered a thought process that helped me realize that there's no shame in having a natural tendency to watch for and notice the *dots* all around me. There's nothing wrong with having a mind that naturally seeks to fit dots together like a puzzle, looking for and interested in knowing if a picture is there waiting to be discovered. I'd always been that way and have never had ill intentions.

I did this as a kid! I have childhood memories of enjoying the challenge of staring at my 1970s popcorn-textured walls until I began to see shapes take form by connecting the pointy dots. (Hopefully, I wasn't spending all that time staring closely lead paint or asbestos.) That mimics the creative process I follow when painting. I didn't stare at the wall as a kid because I was bored; I did it because I was interested. I began to realize that I liked this about myself. I needed to feel free to unleash my authentic abilities in that area, which also drew upon my creativity. If I had ultimately waited for a boss who clearly recognized this natural ability I had, committed themselves to pulling it out of me, and even knew how to do that, I'd still be waiting. You may have heard the idea that our best qualities can also be our worst. It's true! Identify them and find a place for them to shine. (Reminder: don't forget to process this in relation to your story data and analysis.)

Now I know that following an established strategy (in this case, one proven to impact customer satisfaction) and the application of strategic thinking to enable adherence to the strategy is smart. The following simplistic example demonstrates how strategy and strategic decision making impact your ability to manufacture your product:

Sue joined Weight Watchers with a goal to lose 20 pounds so that she feels her best at her daughter's upcoming wedding (i.e., the product she intends to manufacture is herself less 20 pounds). It's lunchtime, and she's short on the groceries she normally eats for the program. Based on what she's learned about quality management, she decides to think strategically. She considers her options for keeping on track. She has bread, butter, cheese, a knife, a pan, and an oven available to her (the dots). She connects those dots to identify two possibilities for her lunch: a grilled cheese sandwich using a pan, or cheese toast using the oven. Now that she has clarified the possibilities, she can decide what to eat for lunch. She chooses the cheese toast based on her Weight Watchers point allowance just as the doorbell rings. Her neighbor, Jessica, has popped over. (An unexpected event has occurred.) Sue is thrown off by Jessica's arrival and suddenly considers Jessica as the customer for lunch. Based on how she was raised and the rung of Maslow's ladder she's sitting on, the belief that she must satisfy her guest and friend overtakes her thought process (although Jessica did pop over uninvited at noon, and Sue has made a serious commitment to manufacturing her product). Sue doesn't know how to satisfy Jessica, so she lets her decide. Later, as Sue eats a grilled cheese sandwich, she realizes that she now has very few Weight Watchers points left for the day. She gets irritated at Jessica, who looks like a string bean. "If she hadn't dropped by uninvited, I'd be eating cheese toast now. Jessica doesn't understand. She can eat whatever she wants. People are always doing this to me." Well, guess what? As the manufacturer for the 5-star product she wants, Sue holds the power to make that happen, not Jessica. Sue's eating a sandwich based on *her* decision *not* to decide. She did not follow through on her initial strategy, which included accepting that she is 100% responsible for her product and sticking to her quality policy. She gave her power to Jessica and then got irritated at her.

When she took the time to identify the resources available to her so that she could continue to follow her strategy, Sue was essentially being opportunistic. She's looked for the opportunities available within her system that would allow her to move forward. If she had decided that she should simply go from neighbor to neighbor asking if they had a Weight Watchers frozen lunch, and expect them to give it to her, she would be going beyond the boundaries of her scope of influence. She would be expecting people and situations she has no control over to resolve her issue.

By letting Jessica decide what she will eat for lunch and by expecting others to provide her with what she wants to eat when she doesn't have it, Sue is throwing her system out of control. She is limiting the ability to ensure that she can manufacture her intended product. She's giving up her power and her ability to have what she wants to have for herself and for her daughter on a special day.

COMMIT OUT LOUD

As discussed in Chapter 3 (which included a section with the same title), corporate leaders commit out loud to the concepts of quality management because they believe in the science. To do that, they create a quality policy, communicate it throughout the organization, and then set the example that they expect employees to follow. When their actions match their words, it works! When they don't, it's like parenting. You can tell your children that honesty is the best policy for 18 years. However, if you continuously demonstrate dishonesty during that time, they may become dishonest people, they may not trust others, or both. Quality *always* starts at the top. In this scenario, you are at the top. To move forward, I choose to assume that your philosophies and mindset related to quality are shifting, and that you're open to continue your move. As this happens, your personal vibe will shift, too. Earlier in the book, I suggested that you think about *personal culture* as your "vibe." Has anyone ever asked something like this about your workplace, "What's the vibe there?" If so, they are essentially asking you to describe the culture.

Years ago, when I was beginning to internalize how quality is managed, I heard an analogy comparing the corporate quality policy to a crystal ball. At an internal leadership meeting, we were told to add this crystal ball to all the others we juggled daily as we made management decisions. Whatever happened, if we maintained our commitment to keeping that crystal ball safe, our decisions would align with upholding the highest priority of our company, which was patient safety. The highest possible levels of quality emerge from that level of commitment, whether related to our daily tasks or our career as a whole/product. Having such a crystal ball provides a framework for decision making. I brought this concept into my personal life and spent a lot of time thinking about having a quality crystal ball I should never drop. That led me to think about what quality meant to *me*. What reality, goal, or vision did I want to protect by keeping it safe? In the context of this book, the crystal ball must not drop so that you can build and then retain 5-star worthy satisfaction in your career. (Last reminder: don't forget to process this in relation to your story data and analysis.)

If you're a spiritual person, you may be thinking that the doctrine you follow is your crystal ball. The crystal ball this book focuses on is specific to how you define quality, and how that informs the quality of your career. On a basic level any spiritual doctrine you may follow plays a role in how you define quality. The concepts described in this book should not create a conflict because this is about *your* definition of quality and how *you* define a 5-star career.. If your career requires you to conduct business or execute tasks that conflict with your religious or moral beliefs, I bet it's not the 5-star career you'd prefer to have.

Considering the difference between objective and subjective data/ information, it would be illogical to share your religious beliefs at work every chance you get, regardless of your company's personnel and/or code of conduct-related policies. You likely agreed to follow the company policies upon hiring. Those policies are not within your scope of influence to change. That they exist, that you signed them, and that changing them is not within the scope of your influence are all objective facts. A belief that your religion is the best (like yellow) is subjective information, owned by you. If you are confused and think that it's objective, and that it's your duty to ensure that everyone at work agrees with you, you're wrong. Each individual gets to choose the religion they believe is best, or choose not to have one. No one will likely care if you mention what you did at church last Sunday, but if you spend half of your day working to convince them to agree that your religion is best, they are not going to be able to focus on their work. They'll grow tired of the conversation, feeling that you are imposing your subjective data onto them, which at some point becomes rude. You have a decision. You can choose to adhere to the company policies or accept that telling others about your religion has authentic importance to you. Perhaps the ability to do that at work is part of how you define a 5-star career. If so, that's fine! You can confidently decide to identify a job/career that enables you to include this element. Again, you're a unique and talented person. You will never have a 5-star career unless you appropriately define what 5-star means to you, and then use the resources available within your scope of influence to go in that direction.

A quality policy is essentially a written commitment to quality. If it would be helpful, flip back to Chapter 3 for a reminder of why it's an important document for organizations. I'm not going to insist that you write a personal quality policy (although you can; I probably would, only because I haven't been able to stop writing since I was about seven). If you're a young adult just getting started, or an empty nester with a job or career that isn't 5-star worthy by your standards, writing it on paper can help solidify your commitment and/or serve to remind you along the way. If you choose to do so, it's a good document to put on your bulletin board at work or at home. Regardless, if you've made the decision to proactively commit to building your 5-star career following the science of quality management, establishing your own quality policy is the first step. If you refer to Figure 7.1, you'll recall that philosophy and mindset essentially dovetail to create corporate culture and personal culture (aka vibe). In Chapter 3, a system was defined as "all the various parts that work together to make something happen." Your goal is to establish a quality policy that can support the development of your 5-star career by serving as your crystal ball. We also defined philosophy as "a set of beliefs or opinions, in a sense, that guides your thoughts about all kind of practical, daily life, scenarios." Your overarching quality policy should reflect the philosophy that drives your career decisions. If asked today, could you immediately describe your personal quality policy? As a young person, my response to this question would have been, "I always strive to do my best!" Several years into my career, my responses would have moved towards, "I manage my time well," and "I focus on meeting the yearly goals my supervisor sets for me." While these are both admirable answers (I did all that for years, as I hung in there at 3 stars), they're nonspecific and would demonstrate a lack of clear understanding of the question. But guess what? Most bosses would say, "That sounds wonderful. You're hired!" It feels like a win-win, right? We're all happy. I have the job. Ten years later, I'm still at 3 stars, and someone is telling me that a plan is not a strategy. Like I said, no one teaches us this stuff.

I encourage you to reflect on your story data and analysis and consider whether you've had any type of personal policy related to quality, and if so, what it was, if it was effective, etc. If so, did it have any bearing on your story? If not, would something like this have shifted any of the decisions you made, or outcomes? I'm sure that it would have influenced my thought process, decisions, and the outcome of my department store debacle. A personal quality policy might be something like the example below. It could be even shorter, or much longer. That's for you to decide:

> I am committed to managing the quality of my career following the proven science of quality management. I'm going to incorporate that commitment into all that I plan, do, and produce; it will weave through every process I have or develop, decision I make, and action I take from this day forward. Given my authentic nature, I acknowledge that this may not always be the easiest thing to do, but I know that it will be the right thing to do.

Creating a mental or written personal commitment to quality and sharing it with your partner, family, best friend, mentor, coworker, boss, etc., is your choice. However, bear in mind that the proven science of quality management includes a step for communicating the policy to those who ultimately will be called upon to support the culture (i.e., vibe) you aim to create. I encourage you to do this when you're ready, even if it feels a bit odd. It's about helping to engage those with whom you interact with the most to understand how important this is to you. It may help them to better understand some of the decisions you make going forward. As an individual, you're not required to explain yourself, or share your personal policies with others; however, the science of quality management tells us that doing so is helpful, especially when it comes to those who have clear and consistent touchpoints with your personal quality system (e.g., they provide inputs to us or receive our output). That's where the quality management concept of collaboration comes into play. (To dive into that, I may need to write another book; I believe this explanation will do for now.)

KEY POINTS

1. You should not let a concern about incomplete or imperfect data paralyze your career or push it in the direction of flying blind. Move forward with the data you have.
2. Regardless of the depth and breadth of your story-related thoughts, this is when you move forward, draw a line in the sand, and start the first day of the rest of your life. You get to decide what to bring with you, and what to leave behind.
3. *Strategy* is defined as a plan of action or policy designed to achieve a major or overall aim.
4. The science of quality management calls for creating a plan *and* thinking strategically as you execute that plan. Why? Because sometimes plans don't go as smoothly as you imagined.
5. Whether you're a teacher, attorney, store manager, or hair stylist, applying strategic thinking to the work that you do and products you contribute to is one of the most valuable skills you can offer.
6. The science of quality management needs a seat at that table. I suggest that quality management is the table, and that if all those pithy, powerful psychological concepts and philosophical idea we've all read about could pull their chair up closer, many of us may gain a heck of a lot more clarity.
7. While *strategy* is more often associated with war, James Bond, corporate intrigue, and political debates, *plan* tends to be associated

with family vacations, teaching curricula, what's for dinner, and what you want to be when you grow up.

8. Following an established strategy (in this case, one proven to impact customer satisfaction) and the application of strategic thinking to enable adherence to the strategy is smart.

11

Claim Your System

"Goals are good for setting direction, but systems are best for making progress."

—James Clear

It's possible that raising a kid takes a village. There's some subjectivity mixed up in this African proverb. It means that an entire community of people must interact with children for them to experience and grow in a safe and healthy environment. I tend to agree with it, but you may not. Choosing is our prerogative. However, it *does* take the science of quality management to have the highest possible assurance that:

- A widget leaves the manufacturing plant and nabs consistent 5-star reviews.
- An FDA-approved medication is safe and effective.
- A flight from Philadelphia safely reaches San Francisco.
- You can wake up one morning knowing that you have a 5-star career.

This book includes quite a bit of material focused on the reality that a wide variety of unique factors influenced who you are today. You have moved through a cornucopia of overlapping, dovetailing, and conflicting subsystems since the day you entered this giant chaotic system where we all must coexist. When you were a child, your personal scope of influence was tiny; you relied on adults to survive. You instinctively reacted to what was happening around you and inside of you (e.g., hunger, exhaustion, pain) until your ability and responsibility to make decisions about how you would respond evolved. You experienced a growing awareness of

DOI: 10.4324/9780367855260-11

the more obvious systems around you such as the educational, legal, healthcare, and political systems, and also your own family unit. There may have been years when your family, high school, or sports teams were your entire world. You may have been either joyfully immersed, standing on the outskirts wanting in, or even feeling trapped in its grip. However, none of that was ever *your* system. As you moved toward adulthood, your personal scope of influence grew.

BORDERS ARE NOT FENCES

You may think that I'm referring to your influence over everything around you, but I'm not. I'm referring to your scope of influence over *yourself*, the ability (i.e., power) to make decisions that lead to the outcomes you want. Although your ability to make decisions grew, your system did not. Objective data and information tell us that an individual's personal system has set borders. Your system and its set borders move with you throughout your life. What grows is your ability to independently manage that system. Figure 11.1 illustrates how an individual's personal system remains consistent as they move from infancy to adulthood. The boxes depict the personal systems of the child and adult. The changing tone of the child's system (i.e., box) represents the increasing ability to control their personal system. Added to this, you see Maslow's hierarchy of needs. Figure 11.1 is a process that I hope you were able to successfully complete on your way to adulthood. The text provides insight into the colliding perspectives at play.

Figure 11.1 shows how we move from physiological dependance on an adult to emerge as an autonomous adult. In industry, a quality management system is a collection of business processes focused on consistently meeting customer requirements and enhancing their satisfaction. It is aligned with an organization's purpose and strategic direction. To maintain control of their quality management system they operate within the defined borders of their system. Your quality management system will include the collection of processes focused on consistently meeting your customer (you) requirements and enhancing satisfaction. The quality management system will align with your purpose, and strategic direction, which is to manufacture a 5-star career. All companies and all people have a system; the key is to transform it into a quality management system

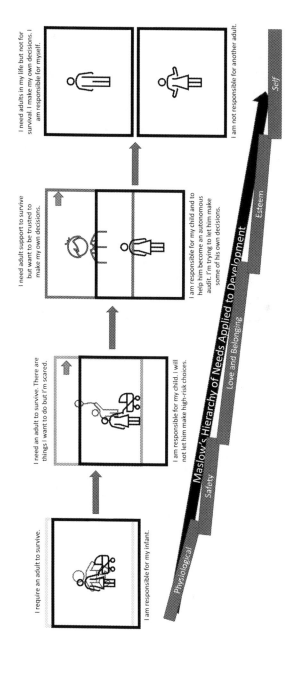

FIGURE 11.1
Child interaction with self-actualized adult.

(i.e., a system focused on managing quality). Yet, this science proven to result in high quality has been relegated to the business realm. Companies across industries that have embraced the science of quality management, understand and accept that working within their own system is the proven route to success. A company can only control its own system Historically, quality management professionals have not actively explored and communicated how the science can also be applied on a personal level to improve quality of life. Just like companies, working within your own system will always work best. You can only control what is yours to control. The trick is understanding what the system is and how to manage it to produce the quality outcomes you want.

Now, let's imagine that the universal biological needs required for a human infant to emerge as a physically and mentally self-actualized adult are not met. In this case, a person enters adulthood (and the workforce) on a lower rung of Maslow's ladder. Figure 11.2 depicts how this can impact their interactions with self-actualized adults.

Now, let's take it one step further and imagine the impact when an adult, whose universal biological needs for self-actualization are not yet met, interacts with an adult in the same boat. Figure 11.3 depicts this scenario, demonstrating that failing to understand the difference between subjective and objective data and information diminishes the ability to control a system. In this scenario, both adults are struggling to have their needs met through variables beyond the borders of their own personal systems. Unfortunately, neither may realize that this is happening. The tone of the box around the adult does not change in this figure because the focus is on the other adult moving toward self-actualization.

In the final Figure 11.3 scenario, you see how an individual, finally self-actualized, may be faced with choosing to build a fence along the southern border of their system; this can be extremely difficult. For example, in my case, if my mother is incapable of change, I have a choice to make. I've learned that, in some cases, there are hard decisions to make when we finally reach self-actualization and intend to stay there. It is my right and your right as biological human creatures to arrive there and stay there. That is an objective fact.

Take a pause to consider the interactions you had with the adults in your life as you were growing up. The adults may have been your parents or others whom you depended on or trusted. Also, consider your adult interactions, both outside and within the context of your career. It may be helpful to look back at your Story Data Mining Tool with this in mind.

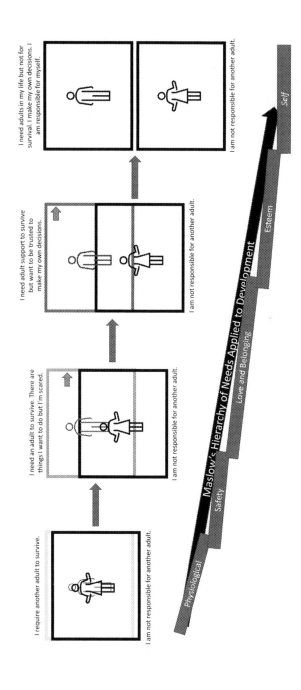

FIGURE 11.2

Adult interaction: not self-actualized and self-actualized.

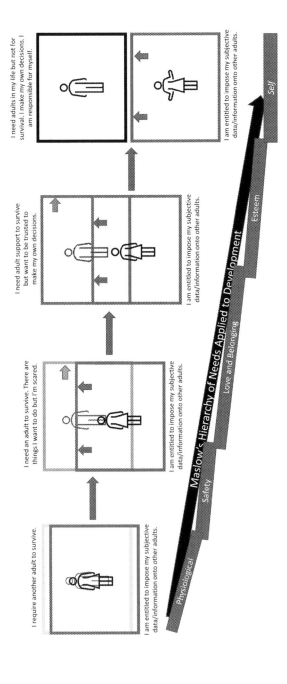

FIGURE 11.3

Adult interactions: not self-actualized.

I could generate pages of figures depicting numerous scenarios between two adults and within group dynamics that can result due to the interplay of the three concepts of focus here:

- An individual's understanding of what defines a personal system and how working within it works.
- An individual's clarity around the difference between objective and subjective information and data.
- Where an individual is on Maslow's hierarchy of needs.

My hope is that you are beginning to accept that you aren't capable of knowing where all the people who come in and out of your life stand on the three elements above or why (i.e., the details of their story). Mix those unknowns with all that you've learned about philosophy, mindset, culture, customer satisfaction, quality, and how to manufacture it, and you'll see undeniable chaos. That level of chaos (and how it goes on and on twisting like a string around a ball, deeper and deeper, beyond everything that you know and have experienced, moving across the world) is why the following high-level process applied within the strategy discussed in Chapter 10 can work based on the proven science of quality management. Consider the process outlined below as the top-level process in your manufacturing plant.

TOP-LEVEL PROCESS FOR CAREER PRODUCTION

1. Identify the product that you will manufacture (e.g., career).
2. Make a commitment to manufacture that career following the science of quality management.
3. Seek to gain a deeper understanding of your customer (you), establishing the career specifications required to result in 5-star customer (you) satisfaction. Uphold a commitment to data integrity.
4. Establish a next-level plan/process specific to the manufacture of that 5-star career that can be executed within your system.
5. Manage and monitor your manufacturing process to ensure that it remains in control and able to generate the 5-star career.
6. Once created, monitor the 5-star career to address the root cause of any dips in satisfaction.

Steps 1 through 3 were the focus of Chapters 1–9. The focus of Chapter 10 was strategizing for quality. The goal of this chapter is to clarify what a personal system is and provide the top-level process for career production (above). Remember the assembly line with 20 subprocesses? The process above is at the level of the manufacturer saying, "We will have an assembly line." Depending on what your 5-star career looks like, you'll need to lay out the next process level (i.e., what are those 20 steps?). This is up to you. It may be that you're happy where you work or with the responsibilities you have, yet it's not 5-star worthy due to the interpersonal situations at play, the commute, the salary, etc. Or you may feel that you're in a 2-star career because you want and need, at an authentic level, to do something different with your time all day. You can't identify the next-level process and its steps until you spend the time required to figure that piece out. What are *your* specifications? If you don't know yet or need additional clarity, I recommended taking the time needed to digest the contents of this book, go back to your Story Data Mining Tool, read it again, analyze your data again, answer the questions again, whatever it takes to establish some level of certainty around what *you* want. You. You. You. No one else is the customer. You may naturally feel compelled to consider the impact that your process may have on those you interact with daily, whether inside or outside of work. I won't sugarcoat it; risk is unavoidable in any scenario. Risk was there before you picked up this book and it's not going away. The great news is that the science of quality management takes that into account. Once you establish as much clarity as possible on the specifications of your 5-star career, you can begin to consider the required process steps and then make decisions based on risk. Chapters 12 and 13 will include assessing risk and making risk-based decisions not only when establishing your process, but also when your process is challenged.

SIMPLE IS NOT ALWAYS EASY

You must always begin where you are with what you have. In industry, according to long-held business theories and even the law, responsibility ultimately lies at the top levels of management. In Fortune 500 companies, this is one of the major reasons why paychecks get larger as the scope of responsibility widens. Many people complain about the high salaries of corporate c-suite executives. I won't comment on salary bands, but I will point out that sitting at the tip top of a gigantic global company such as Pfizer, Microsoft, or General Electric must carry an incredible intellectual and emotional load. I admire anyone who can bear that burden daily and not crumble. Being in that position is a lot to ask of anyone. Could you do it? Would you choose to do it, and if so, what compensation would you seek in return? I'm sure that there are people out there who would say that you couldn't pay them a billion dollars to take that job. At this point, it's imperative to forget about those CEOs and the job, salary, etc., of anyone else you know. That's all part of that giant, crazy ball of chaos string. If you get wrapped up in exposing or untying the knots of others, you'll likely never even flip the light switch in your own manufacturing plant. If you focus on beginning where you are at this moment and apply the quality management strategy and top-level process I've shared, you'll move toward your 5-star career whether that includes being CEO for a Fortune 50 company, being a bestselling author, working to change corporate compensation standards, saving lives every day as an emergency medical technician, or teaching 2nd grade.

I hear you. Why can't it be easy! There's a difference between simple and easy. In his great article, "Decomplication: How to Find Simple Solutions to 'Hard' Problems," author and entrepreneur, Nat Eliason, wrote, "Running a marathon is simple because you just run, but it is not easy." I highly recommend finding this article online and reading it.

It doesn't seem fair that some people are required to make a heck of a lot less decisions to get what they want. I mean, things would be different ...

- If I'd a better boss for the last five years.
- If I didn't have to work with backstabbers, irresponsible people, or people who constantly distract me.
- If I didn't live in such an economically depressed area.
- If I'd gone to a better high school, technical school, or college.
- If I had another degree.
- If I had enough time and money to make the changes I want to make.

Plus, I'm clearly at a disadvantage between these natural borders of mine ...

- I'm a gray-haired white male approaching retirement.
- I'm a woman and my voice doesn't carry.

- I'm black.
- I'm white.
- I'm too young.
- I'm too old.
- I have a disability.
- I grew up in a bubble in Malibu. My parents didn't prepare me for the real world. They tried to buy my way into Harvard and didn't even tell me! I have no clue how the real world works. People look at me, and my nice clothes, and make assumptions; they don't see *me*. I'm not sure I see myself. I'm trying to figure out who I am. I'm so confused.
- I grew up in inner-city Philadelphia. No one prepared me for the real world. I had to learn how to take care of myself, even when I was hungry. People look at me, listen to my accent, and make inaccurate assumptions; they don't see how real I am. I *think* I know who I want to be, but I don't know how to be that person. Sometimes it feels hopeless.

How can you possibly scale that growing mountain of disadvantage, especially if you're to work within borders, you know, the ones they showed you? *Who* showed you? Your parents? The people in your neighborhood or cultural region? Your favorite actor or 24-hour news personality? Your friends, brilliant college professor, or the author of those books you read? In the context of quality management, forget all that. You may care about them. You may admire them or even love them. Your ability and right to care, admire, and love who and what you choose is subjective data that is yours. Regardless, they are *not* the manufacturer of your life, your personal system, or your career. You are 100% responsible. Just as if you were given the position of heading up global manufacturing for Apple, you must make your *own* commitment to quality, walk onto *your* manufacturing floor, work within your system, and make *it* happen. If you landed the Apple job, would you call your mom, friend, or professor expecting them to tell you everything you need to know about the Apple manufacturing system and exactly what you should do to achieve the company's goals? Would you later be upset with them if the information and advice they provided turned out to be wrong? No, because it's not their job. It's not their system. It's not their responsibility. It's yours, and that is incredibly exciting once you recognize the personal power that brings.

One of the tough skills I had to hone during my career is how best to deliver not-so-great news to all kinds of people at all levels of management, while simultaneously helping them realize that it's good news. The positive message is that they now know what needs to be done to increase the probability of achieving their goals. I must be willing and able to, with confidence, look into the eyes of the scariest, meanest, most negative person I've ever met, or an incredibly emotional person already crying gigantic, stress-filled tears (if that's the case), and tell them that something they're doing is incorrect, not good enough, etc., and why. Over many years, I developed a good approach. So, here's my tough news *for you*: I'd be doing you a disservice, stealing the money you paid for this book and the time you used to read it, if I don't tell you that, unfortunately, the world will *never* be fair. It is an unpredictable, chaotic system filled with trillions of variables; it is out of control. I don't care who you are, expecting to achieve anything worthwhile without running into adversity along the way is unrealistic. This includes you, and anyone else you can possibly think of, regardless of what types of decisions they are required to make within their personal system. And every single one of those people is working their way up Maslow's ladder of needs, whether they know it or not.

Working within your system is what will work. Understanding your system, the difference between objective and subjection data and information, having a strategy founded on the science of quality management, and focusing on control of that system is where your power lies. Forget about where anyone else's power lies. It's irrelevant and a waste of your time. Don't waste another second. Another thing you will never know is how much time is in your bank, and exactly when it will run dry. By incorporating quality management concepts more intrinsically into your world over time, the quality of your career can improve in a self-directed way that puts you in the driver's seat rather than feeling that you're dependent on any number of factors beyond your control. As employees, we are tasked with "getting things done," whether related to specific assigned duties or managing the work of others. Consider yourself tasked with the full responsibility and power to manage your own career. In the end, there will be an outcome, a product, and it's *your* quality rating that counts. I challenge you to take responsibility with gusto, rather than waiting, hoping, or depending on outcomes that you have no control over.

CONTROL QUALITY AT EVERY STEP

Earlier, I shared that a good general definition of *process* is a series of logically related activities or tasks (such as planning, production, or sales) performed together to produce a defined set of results. During product development, manufacturers think through the life cycle of a product in terms of small, interrelated processes. It highlights how one process affects the quality of the next. In a process-focused environment, staff members are trained to think in terms of how their work affects the quality of the processes that follow. Again, the assembly line with 20 steps is a good example for this. This results in an ongoing push for high-quality inputs and outputs each time processes intersect, which results in the final product meeting the required specifications.

Keeping that in mind, let's assume you're ready for Step 4 in the process below.

TOP-LEVEL PROCESS FOR CAREER PRODUCTION

1. Identify the product that you will manufacture (e.g., career).
2. Make a commitment to manufacture that career following the science of quality management.
3. Seek to gain a deeper understanding of your customer (you), establishing career specifications required to result in 5-star customer (you) satisfaction. Uphold a commitment to data integrity.
4. **Establish a next-level plan/process specific to the manufacture of that 5-star career that can be executed within your system.**
5. Manage and monitor your manufacturing process to ensure that it remains in control and able to generate the 5-star career.
6. Once created, monitor the 5-star career to address the root cause of any dips in satisfaction.

Your next-level process will be highly specific to you and your 5-star career specifications. For that reason, the most helpful approach I can take is to provide some additional information about the nature of processes. Following that, you will need to take the time to consider what specific steps to include in your next level process and why. Each step should produce an output that contributes to the next step, as well as your final product (just like an assembly line). Try not to get trapped by thinking that you can't predict the future. Anything can happen! Although you may be thinking about risk, and we will focus on that in Chapters 12 and 13, I urge you to table that until we get there. Once a manufacturer has clarity on their product, they develop process steps that will result in the product. They can't predict the future either. What they are doing is using science to drive the future that they envision, and they do this all within the borders of their system. This means that as the manufacturer of your product, you will map out a process that includes steps that lead to outcomes that you can control within the scope of your quality system.

Table 11.1 provides examples of two simple processes. Sally's process includes three steps for which the outcomes are within her personal control. Bob's process starts out well but moves beyond his personal quality system at Step 3. He cannot control the outcome of Step 3; it will only work out if he's lucky. The probability that he will get a new car using his process is much lower than Sally's. If it does work, he may end up in one of the scenarios depicted in Figures 11.2 and 11.3. Taking his approach is *one* way that many people end up in careers that they rate less than 5 stars, regardless of what anyone else would rate it.

In developing controlled processes, it's critical to design steps for which you can control the outcome, including the quality of the output that contributes to the next step. We'll look at this in a different context in Chapter 12.

TABLE 11.1

Example of Two Simple Processes Designed with Differing Approaches

Product	Sally's Process Process that Remains within Her System (She Can Control This)	Bob's Process Process that Moves beyond His System (He Can't Control This)
A car	1) Make a budget that includes a car payment 2) Determine how much additional money is needed per month 3) Decide to cut something out of existing budget to shift funds to a car payment, or increase monthly earnings by accepting the part-time position Old Navy offered me this week 4) Accept the Old Navy position ...	1) Make a budget that includes a car payment 2) Determine how much additional money is needed per month 3) Make a list of my relatives who will each give me $50.00 a month for a while since they make more money than I do and would really want me to have a decent car. (Maybe a relative will just give me one of their cars!) 4) Figure out my pitch to the relatives ...

THE MOUNTAIN HAS MULTIPLE PATHS

As you consider the process steps that can take you where you want to go following the concepts of quality management, it's important to accept that there may be numerous routes one can take. You must decide which steps/route is going to work best for you. To demonstrate that more than one process can be followed to create a product, let's look at how two artists approach painting a portrait of a child. The following example provides insight into other aspects of process design that may be helpful to consider. If you recall, just like systems, there is always a process at play. Even if you achieve the same goal following a unique approach each time, you still followed a process. It may seem odd, but *not* having a process may be your process. To demonstrate, I'll use painting an original portrait of a child. Table 11.2 includes the high-level process steps for two talented artists: Tim and Julie.

TABLE 11.2

High-Level Processes Followed by Two Talented Artists for the Creation of a Child's Portrait

Step	Artist 1 (Tim)	Artist 2 (Julie)
1	Obtain several photos of client's child	Cut some canvas off a canvas roll and pin it to the wall of art studio
2	Select wrapped canvas in size specified by client	Randomly grab four or five colors that *call* to you
3	Create detailed drawing of child on canvas	Select one color and apply it haphazardly to canvas with an old paintbrush that was rarely cleaned
4	Paint drawing of child and background using the color palette specified by the client; follow highly technical steps using skills obtained in Master of Fine Arts degree program.	Turn on the Bee Gee's *Greatest Hits* and begin painting whatever comes to mind
5	Review and make final adjustments	Step back and look for an image within the chaos
6	Apply appropriate finish to protect the painting	Once spotted, work to illuminate/clarify the image; add details and background
Product	**Portrait of a child**	**Portrait of a child**

Both artists may believe that Julie doesn't follow a process. However, Julie may consider that her approach *is* a process she consistently follows. Tim may believe that he follows the correct process because it's what he learned in a master's level art program, and art critics praise his technical skills. Both processes resulted in a child's portrait. Which process is better? That's tough to answer without having more information, such as:

1. What are the expectations of the client whose child is the subject of Portrait 1? Did the customer ask for a highly technical hyper-realistic portrait?
2. If the customer who commissioned Portrait 1 was also the customer for Portrait 2, did the artist know the child?
3. Did either Tim or Julie subconsciously deem *themselves* the customer?

This example not only demonstrates how the perception of *no process* is often incorrect, it also demonstrates the importance of purpose, scope, and roles within a process. Let's look at the questions above again. Understanding customer expectations, scope, and roles is necessary to determine if a process is generally on track versus completely off the rails.

1. **What were the expectations of the customer whose child was the subject of Tim's portrait? Did the customer ask for a highly technical hyper-realistic portrait?**
   If the customer expected Tim's portrait to be hyper-realistic using a specified palette, this process seems to work. If the customer expected the portrait to be a whimsical, imaginative portrait capturing the inner spirit of the child, the process falls short. If the customer had no idea what they wanted, it was a gamble on Tim's part; he had to make some decisions on his own. He had no framework in which to work. Perhaps Tim forgot to ask questions? Perhaps he made assumptions about what the client wanted? If so, he introduced several risks to his success.
   Also, if Tim decided to ditch a color palette selected by the client and use colors he loves, he failed to maintain a consistent focus on his customer's specifications. Tim made the error of believing that the colors he chose were better than the colors that the customer specified. In this case, Tim does not understand the nature of subjective data.

2. **If the customer who commissioned Portrait 1 also commissioned Portrait 2, did Julie know the child?**

As with Tim's portrait, Julie's masterpiece may be what the customer asked for, knowing that the artist had spent a lot of time with the child. However, if a hyper-realistic portrait like Tim's was expected, the client will be disappointed.

3. **Did Tim and/or Julie subconsciously or consciously view themselves as the customer?**

If an artist does not have a specific customer in mind and paints for their own enjoyment or expression, either approach could work well. The process developed reflects the artist and leads to original art that visually portrays not only a subject but the artist.

However, if Julie dreams of painting hyper-realistic portraits, her process doesn't appear optimal. She may need to seriously consider how her process can be adjusted/improved to produce the result/ product that will satisfy her. If Julie continues to follow the same process every time, proclaiming that this is *the way it's done*, or this is *the way she's always done it*, or this is the way that her Aunt Polly, who was a famous artist in the 1960s, told her to do it, progress will be extremely slow. Even if it makes perfect sense to me and every person who reads this book, Julie may be blind to the fact that hyper-realistic art may not be what she's authentically gifted at creating. She may be following a carrot that looks like her Aunt Polly. Julie is gifted at creating highly emotional, expressive art! Once this is clear to her and she accepts that it's okay to toss that carrot aside, Julie's career can move to the next level.

Similarly, if Tim's dream has always been to paint large hyper-realistic commissioned works for wealthy patrons, he's on the right track. However, if he does not accept that switching the agreed-upon palette is not acceptable to his customer, his career may flounder. Tim may be lying in bed at night, telling himself, "I just don't understand these people! The painting is amazing with the palette I chose. What a jerk! I did all that work and produced an amazing piece of art. Now the client is telling me it's not good enough! I'm the artist! They don't understand what it is to be an artist!" If so, Tim also has a blind spot that is preventing progress.

KEY POINTS

1. Your system and its set borders move with you throughout your life. What grows is your ability to independently manage that system.

2. All companies and all people have a system; the key is to transform it into a quality management system (i.e., a system focused on managing quality).

3. In some cases, there are hard decisions to make when we finally reach self-actualization and intend to stay there. It is my right and your right as biological human creatures to arrive there and stay there.

4. If you get wrapped up in exposing or untying the knots of others, you'll likely never even flip the light switch in your own manufacturing plant.

5. The world will *never* be fair. It is an unpredictable, chaotic system filled with trillions of variables; it is out of control. I don't care who you are, expecting to achieve anything worthwhile without running into adversity along the way is unrealistic.

6. Working within your system is what will work. Understanding your system and the difference between objective and subjection data and information, having a strategy founded on the science of quality management, and focusing on control of that system is where your power lies.

7. Once a manufacturer has clarity on their product, they develop process steps that will result in the product. They can't predict the future. What they are doing is using science to drive the future that they envision, and they do this all within the borders of their system.

8. In developing controlled processes, it's critical to design steps for which you can control the outcome, including the quality of the output that contributes to the next step.

12

Design Your Process

"We should work on our process, not the outcome of our processes."

—W. Edwards Deming

Although depicted as boxes in the Chapter 11 figures, your personal system can't be defined by space or time. I think of it as a dimension in which an individual can mold the future by careful and deliberate decision making. Once you recognize the power you have to operate within that dimension, you can use it to manufacture the future you desire. If you're thinking that this sounds a bit manipulative or opportunistic, remember that identifying and taking opportunities and making choices that will lead to an ending you prefer is okay in the context of quality management. You are operating within your own personal system, which includes making decisions based on your ability to impact outcomes.

DECISIONS. DECISIONS.

In the science of quality management, the term *specifications* refers to two aspects of product manufacturing. It refers to the product attributes that will satisfy the intended customer. It also refers to specific elements required to produce the product. For example, if the product must be frozen, *frozen* is a specification of the product. The manufacturer must identify the specific elements (i.e., specifications) required to produce a frozen product. Table 12.1 includes several career-related examples of a potential career requirement. If each of these were your specifications, you must ask yourself if you can fulfil the requirement given *your* resources.

DOI: 10.4324/9780367855260-12

TABLE 12.1

How to Think When Creating Your High-Level Process: Three Examples of Assessing Current Resources

Career Specification	Example Potential Requirement (i.e., Specification)	Can I Make This Happen Using the Resources within My Scope Today?
Involves tasks and responsibilities that are creative	Create an art portfolio	Yes
Involves being an attorney	**Obtain a law degree**	**No**
Involves working with children	Position financially to support a career move	Yes

A *yes* answer enables you to move forward independently if you so choose. Let's look at the situation where a law degree is required but you simply can't afford it. Does that mean you must give up? No, you may still have options. In this example, the options aren't too difficult to recognize; however, this step often calls for creative thinking, research, and an open mind. Unfortunately, there are scenarios when you will simply not have an option, which can be heartbreaking. For example, I have a nephew who played college football. He was on a solid road to the NFL, which was his lifelong dream. After three serious concussions, he was told that he could not and should not ever play football again. It was a devastating objective fact. That is what I refer to as a career quality event. You heard this phrase when I shared my story of being laid off by Johnson & Johnson. Later in this chapter, I'll focus on how the science of quality management also provides a proven approach for addressing quality events.

Getting back to your requirement for a law degree and your inability to fund it, Table 12.2 takes you through the next step, which is identifying any additional options you may have for covering the cost of law school, the potential risks for each option, and whether you can accept those or not. As you read through the content in the table, notice that I have identified each statement as objective or subjective. Recall that objective data and information are irrefutable; if you deny it, exclude it from this process, or believe that you can change/control it, you will be feeding yourself a line of bull. It is what it is. Subjective data and information are yours. You own it; you can change it. Lastly, notice that I have circled a key statement.

In Scenario 1, given the associated risks and your willingness to accept some of them, deciding which option to go forward with may not be too

TABLE 12.2

How to Think When Creating Your High-Level Process: How to Obtain a Law Degree When Lacking Personal Financial Resources

What Are My Options?	What Risks Are Associated with This Option?	Am I Willing to Accept This Risk? Why/Why Not? Scenario 1	Am I Willing to Accept This Risk? Why/Why Not? Scenario 2
Get a student loan to attend law school	• I will leave law school with debt (*objective*) • I will have to pay interest on the loan (*objective*)	Yes, student loans are available for this purpose (*objective*)	No, I vowed to never have student debt. It's bad to have student debt (*subjective*)
Work toward a career that does not require that I be an attorney, that I can also deem 5-star worthy	• I will never be an attorney (*objective*)	No, being an attorney is my lifelong dream (*subjective*). I don't have to be an attorney; my life does not depend on it. However, the urge/desire feels so much a part of me that I can't fathom it ever changing. It means more to me than I can say	No, the most successful people I know are attorneys and I'm incredibly interested in the work that they do. I want to be a part of that and be a leader in my chosen field (*subjective*)
Ask my 85-year-old Grammy to fund my law degree. I will pay her back after I graduate	• It is not Grammy's responsibility to fund my law education (*objective*) • She can say no (*subjective*) • My parents may get angry if they find out (*subjective*) • She could be offended (*subjective*) • She could say yes, give me all her money (*subjective*), and not be able to support herself (*objective*)	No, this option goes against my quality policy (*objective*), and the science of quality management. Grammy's ability to give me money is outside my personal system (*objective*); it's unreliable, and too far beyond my control (*objective*). Plus, it doesn't feel like the *right* thing to do, given that she's 85 years old (*subjective*)	No, this option goes against my quality policy (*objective*), and the science of quality management. I don't think Grammy can afford it (*objective*); it's unreliable, and too far beyond my control (*objective*)

(Continued)

TABLE 12.2 (CONTINUED)

How to Think When Creating Your High-Level Process: How to Obtain a Law Degree When Lacking Personal Financial Resources

What Are My Options?	What Risks Are Associated with This Option?	Am I Willing to Accept This Risk? Why/Why Not? Scenario 1	Am I Willing to Accept This Risk? Why/Why Not? Scenario 2
	• She could pass away before I finish school or before I can I repay her (*objective*)		
	• I may feel guilty for asking her (*subjective*)		
	• I may be stressed all the time about this arrangement (*subjective*)		
Join the military program that includes paying for law school	• I will have to stay in the military for x number of years (*objective*)	Yes	No, I'm not comfortable with the idea of serving in the military for these and other reasons (*subjective*)
	• I may be deployed somewhere considered a security risk by the US government (*objective*)		
	• I will be required to handle firearms in my training and to get physically fit (*objective*)		

difficult; you can see that there is a way! Scenario 2, on the other hand, presents a challenge. You cannot accept any of the associated risks, so your options have run dry. Oh, no! This is terrible. Unfair. Maybe you can just swallow your pride and ask Grammy for the money after all? Even if you're not proud of how you got it, you'll still get the degree, right? I mean your quality policy is not (really) *objective*, right? You can change it. You can choose to stop following it. Your choice to stick to it, to decide how committed you will be to it, is *subjective*; however, be reminded that the science of quality management is *objective*. Its effectiveness has been proven consistently over the last 100 plus years. Just like you can choose to refuse your coworker's opinion that red is the best color there is and that you are correct when you chose yellow, you can choose to reject the science of quality management and go your own way. In both cases, you will simply be wrong. Again, I would be doing you a disservice if I didn't make this clear. The color that you think is best *is* best, the color that your coworker thinks is best *is also* best, and the application of the science I've shared with you *will* ensure customer satisfaction. Your quality policy and commitment to following the science of quality management is the crystal ball that cannot drop. Dropping any other ball can be addressed (which we'll cover later in this chapter). Holding onto your crystal ball will steer you toward the best choice, especially during times when it seems that you have none. It points you back to the underlying concepts of quality management:

1. Life is not a process nor is your career. Your career is a *product* created by your process.
2. Quality is defined by the customer; the quality of your product (career/life) is defined by you.
3. Quality cannot be accurately rated or improved until it's defined.
4. You are 100% responsible for your product.

CRYSTAL BLUE PERSUASION

When it seems like all your options have run out, I urge you to make the conscious choice to strengthen your grip on that crystal blue ball. Let's imagine that it has a blue tint because it fits well with the classic 1968 tune, "Crystal Blue Persuasion," by Tommy James and the Shondells. Associating colors, stories, and music with all of this can help you to remember what you're reading (that's been proven, as well). If you've never heard the song, I encourage you to find it on the Internet. When the song was released, many fans thought that the lyrics were inspired by drug use; however, it was confirmed in a 1985 *Hitch Magazine* interview that James' lyrics were inspired while he was reading the Book of Isaiah and Revelations, which tell of a future age of brotherhood of mankind, living in peace and harmony. For that reason, it seems like a good theme song to remind you that holding that crystal blue ball can steer you towards the career that will offer you greater peace and harmony with who you are as an authentic individual, and thus provide 5-star satisfaction. The song has music with a feel-good, groovy flow, and lyrics that include the sun rising, a new day coming, and people changing. The song tells us to get ready to see the light, not to give up, and to open our minds at times when we are not sure what to do. Hold tight, remember this soothing tune, and then have the courage to do what's next (which I'll explain next).

USE YOUR POWER TO CREATE OPTIONS

The times in my life when I've felt the most hopeless, including when I downed my mother's medications at 19 years old, have been when I believed that I had no options, no way out, no road away from what I didn't want, or toward something that I desperately wanted. I suspect that is how my brother, John, felt standing in his yard on Lost Lake Lane with a gun pointed to his head. There aren't words to describe or define the depth of his tragedy. I know this, particularly because I have perfect clarity on what would have been lost had I died at 19. Over the many years I spent recovering from that dark place, I've decided that hopelessness is a real emotion. I will never tell someone feeling hopeless that there is hope. It's like saying that the emotion they feel isn't real. In that moment, they don't have hope. Hope is not something they can feel, and they desperately need someone to understand that. The worst, darkest level of hopelessness is an extremely difficult emotion to explain or express. Now that I also know what grief feels like, I can say that it's similarly indescribable. I've learned that in a state of hopelessness, it's more helpful to accept the lack of hope, and instead focus on the courage to keep moving *without* hope, even if it feels like you're walking in the dark looking for the door. Courage can take you to another place. I know personally that there is a door to be found, and when you find it, you also find hope again.

However, if you find yourself in a situation like Scenario 2 in Table 12.2, you are not in *that* situation. You may be stuck behind a blind spot, but you are not in the dark. You're in a situation that continues to hold viable options you can take to meet your goal of attending law school. This is where the rubber hits the road in your understanding of objective versus subjective data and information. You *cannot* change the objective information. You *can* change *your* subjective data and information that informed your initial decisions. You can change it because it belongs to you. It's critical to understand that you have no control over Granny's subjective data or information. If you refuse to give up on earning a law degree, your option is to reconsider each subjective statement and consider if you are open and willing to change your mind. In many cases, this may require stepping outside of your comfort zone (not your personal system), so that you can earn that degree and manufacture the 5-star career that you want.

This is good news! You have the power to pick up the magic subjectivity wand waiting for you in that exciting dimension called your personal system, and change. Waving that wand will give you back every option in Table 12.2, except the Grammy option. Remember, choosing Grammy will break your crystal ball, throwing your quality system out of control. Not an option, ever. Don't even consider it.

If you refuse to reconsider the subjective aspects of your decision, or choose not to change it, you will need to accept that you aren't going to earn a law degree. You can then spend your life being upset about this, or you can work on developing 5-star career specifications that do not include having a law degree (which is another option included in Table 12.2; you're allowed to change your mind or rethink the details or your 5-star career at any time. That may be necessary as you fine-tune what you really truly want, and this process can help you do that).

Let's look at Table 12.3 to see how this works.

Sometimes we hesitate to accept risk because we don't realize how much power we have over our own lives. There are deeply personal decisions to be made. Managing quality not only requires making them, but also accepting 100% responsibility for those decisions. Nobody told me this stuff as a kid, a teen, or a young adult. I'm telling you now and you get

TABLE 12.3

How to Think When Creating Your High-Level Process: How to Create Additional Options by Challenging Your Subjective Data

What Are My Options?	What Risks Are Associated with This Option?	Am I Willing to Accept This Risk? Why/Why Not? Scenario 2	How Options Are Created by Questioning/Challenging Your Subjective Data
Get a student loan to attend law school	• I will leave law school with debt (*objective*) • I will have to pay interest on the loan (*objective*)	No, I vowed to never have student debt. It's bad to have student debt (*subjective*)	I can still do this because my vow and belief that student debt is bad is subjective. I will consider the objective facts about taking student loans. Whether it's good or bad is an opinion. Who told me it is bad? Do I think that because someone I know has a lot of student debt? Student debt doesn't have to be a bad thing, if I manage it, pay my bills on time when I graduate, and live within my means. Maybe it's worth the effort if it will enable me to go to law school
Work toward a career that does not require me to be an attorney, that I can also deem 5-star worthy	• I will never be an attorney (*objective*)	No, the most successful people I know are attorneys and I'm incredibly interested in the work that they do. I want to be a part of that and be a leader in my chosen field (*subjective*).	Given that I can do anything I choose with my life, let me rethink this. Must I have a law degree to have a career in the legal system? What other careers might I consider? There are successful people in all careers. I'm interested in the law; maybe I should consider being a police officer, or any number of other professions that involve law

(Continued)

TABLE 12.3 (CONTINUED)

How to Think When Creating Your High-Level Process: How to Create Additional Options by Challenging Your Subjective Data

What Are My Options?	What Risks Are Associated with This Option?	Am I Willing to Accept This Risk? Why/Why Not? Scenario 2	How Options Are Created by Questioning/Challenging Your Subjective Data
Ask my 85-year-old Grammy to fund my law degree. I will pay her back after I graduate	• It is not Grammy's responsibility to fund my law education (*objective*) • She can say no (*subjective*) • My parents may get angry if they find out (*subjective*) • She could be offended • She could say yes, give me all her money (*subjective*), and not being able to support herself (*objective*) • She could pass away before I finish school or before I can I repay her (*objective*) • I may feel guilty for asking her (*subjective*) • I may be stressed all the time about this arrangement (*subjective*)	No, this option goes against my quality policy (*objective*), and the science of quality management. I don't think Grammy can afford it (*objective*); it's unreliable, and too far beyond my control (*objective*)	Still not an option for me. I am committed to following my personal quality policy, which is based on the science of quality management

(Continued)

TABLE 12.3 (CONTINUED)

How to Think When Creating Your High-Level Process: How to Create Additional Options by Challenging Your Subjective Data

What Are My Options?	What Risks Are Associated with This Option?	Am I Willing to Accept This Risk? Why/Why Not? Scenario 2	How Options Are Created by Questioning/Challenging Your Subjective Data
Join the military program that includes paying for law school	• I will have to stay in the military for x number of years (*objective*) • I may be deployed somewhere considered a security risk by the US government. (*objective*) • I will be required to handle firearms in my training and to get physically fit (*objective*)	No, I'm not comfortable with the idea of serving in the military for these and other reasons (*subjective*)	It's hard but I'm going to have an open mind about this. Maybe it's not so bad. Maybe I'm just afraid of it because I have a few relatives who had bad experiences in combat, and my mother cries if anyone ever mentions the possibility. They chose combat positions; I want to be an attorney. It would be nice to attend law school free of charge. I need to do what is best for me and what can support the manufacture of my 5-star career. My mom can't make decisions for me. I'm an adult

to decide whether you will embrace it or continue as is and see what life happens to bring. You have the power to choose your every action; however, there are consequences. Consider these examples:

- You can run out into traffic if you want to do that, but you may get hit by a car. No one is stopping you. You decide! Is that what you want to do?
- Lack of available jobs in your town? You *can* move. What will happen if you move? Oh, you don't have enough money to move your belongings. You can still move. Leave your belongings behind and move. Start fresh. Oh, that's scary? Okay, well just stay then and keep looking for a job. Is that what you want to do? If so, you are making that decision so stand by it and stop being miserable. If you're miserable, then move.
- You want to eat a steak tonight? Okay, then eat a steak. Oh, you can't afford it. Okay, well, that tells you that you'd like to be able to afford a steak. What are you going to do about that? Decide. If you want a steak that bad, then you must take actions that will enable you to eat a steak when you want to eat a steak. If you don't care about the steak that much, then stop wishing you had a steak; you're wasting time. Stop thinking that someone else might stop by and hand you a steak. You have the power to get yourself a steak if that's what you want.
- You want to be promoted but your boss says that the company doesn't need another associate director. If you know you're capable and that's what you want, you can still get that promotion. You'll just have to be an associate director at another company. Start looking. Oh, but you like your coworkers. Maybe you can get promoted in another year, right. If you're ready now, it's your choice. This happened to me. I was even told that our industry doesn't often have a lot of associate director-level positions. Rather than accepting that, I did my own investigation. Within a couple of months, I resigned. I had a new associate director position at Johnson & Johnson. I went out and got it for myself.

The key point is that, as an adult, you can literally do whatever you want to do today, this month, this year, and throughout your life. No one needs to empower you; you already have power. A common thing kids said when I was growing up was, "You're not the boss of me!" Kids have a lot of bosses, but adults do not. Adults only have consequences. I recently heard that decisions are about giving up something you want for something that you want more. It's time to start deciding what you want more than some of the other things you want or may already have.

Once you go through the activity described above to establish the high-level steps you will follow to build your 5-star career, you can create detailed processes for each of the high-level steps. Your high-level steps represent the steps that occur during the product assembly. This is akin to the assembly line example. Each of those steps should have an intended outcome that moves you and/or your career to the next step. You can develop a more detailed process intended to produce the outcome of that major step. You can design detailed subprocesses or you can choose to focus on your high-level steps. Some of your high-level steps may not need a detailed process and some may. Keep in mind that the proven concept is that controlling the quality of each outcome along the assembly line contributes to the quality of the final product.

EXPECT SURPRISES

In the manufacturing process guided by the science of quality management, once a manufacturer has designed a process to create a product, they identify potential variations that can influence the process, and therefore, the product. Variation is one of the most fundamental elements of product manufacturing. Understanding and accounting for types and sources for variation when developing new medications, vaccines, and medical devices is required by regulatory agencies. This topic can get incredibly complex. The complexity increases along with the severity of the risk associated with a defective product being provided to a customer. In the context of manufacturing a 5-star career, a general understanding of variation and how to manage it is required to ensure that your quality management system remains in control.

Let's assume that you've established a high-level process to manufacture your 5-star career. As you initiate that process, regardless of the timeframe it covers (i.e., weeks, months, or years), you must be prepared to recognize, categorize, and address process variations. To ensure that your process will manufacture the intended product, it must remain in control. As the manufacturer, it's your responsibility to keep that control intact despite variations that occur. As mentioned earlier, when developing the process, control can be built in by ensuring that you are able to control the outcome of each step. Asking Granny to fund your law degree is an example of a process step in which you cannot control the outcome and that is packed with risk that you cannot manage.

Unfortunately, designing a process that you are capable of controlling is not enough. Once the process begins, you will no doubt run into variation. W. Edwards Deming, who you may remember from Chapter 2, along with a statistician named Walter Shewhart defined two distinct causes of process variation: common and special.

Common cause variations are those that are to be generally expected, similar to how weight slightly varies from day to day. Most people do not expect to weigh exactly the same, down to the ounce, every day. They expect some level of variation. Common cause variation can be quantified. For example, you may expect variation in how many tasks are on your to-do list on a daily basis. You could also quantify this variation and account for it in your planning. We naturally factor this type of variation into our thought process. If someone asks you how long it will take to write a particular report, you don't spit out that it takes exactly 5 hours, 17 minutes, and 32 seconds. You know that the time naturally varies. Due to this, you're comfortable answering that writing the report takes 5 or so hours. You also know that whether the report takes 5 hours and 15 minutes to write or 4 hours and 52 minutes to write does not have a significant impact on the report quality. No one is going to ask you to prove that. Whereas manufacturers of approved medications are required to understand the common variations in their process and prove that within certain limits, variation of each component does not significantly impact the product.

Special cause variations are surprises. These are new, unanticipated occurrences within the system that have the potential to impact the control of your process, and its ability to deliver the intended process. In manufacturing, methods to identify potential signals of unanticipated variation are used. If a new variation is identified, the manufacturer seeks to uncover the cause of the variation so that it can be fully understood and addressed. Doing this is quite technical on the manufacturing floor.

When monitoring your 5-star career process for special cause variation (i.e., surprises), there's no need to get highly technical. However, variations must be addressed to maintain control of your personal quality system. You know these surprises happen! Unexpected circumstances pop up that can throw you off track and/or derail your plan. When this happens, you're often required to make decisions, some of which can be incredibly difficult. These are the times when you must hold tight to your crystal ball (i.e., quality policy), and rely on strategic thinking and decision making to maintain control of your personal quality system. Examples of special cause variations that can impact your 5-star career process and, therefore, your career itself are:

- Being included in a surprise company lay off
- An unplanned pregnancy
- A new boss who decides to reorganize
- A new coworker who is *extremely* difficult to work with
- A major weather event that impacts your company or industry
- A new company policy stating that tuition reimbursement will end
- Personal illness, or that of a family member
- A virus (e.g., COVID-19)
- A major economic shift (e.g., 2008 mortgage situation)

Earlier, I referred to these types of surprises as career quality events. I noted that the science of quality management includes an approach proven to effectively deal with these unexpected, uncontrollable events. Going forward, you should never again allow a career quality event to convince you that your life and/or your career is merely a series of events happening to you for some mysterious reason that will someday be revealed. Now you know that they are products that you have the power to mold.

KEY POINTS

1. In the science of quality management, the term *specifications* refers to two aspects of product manufacturing. It refers to the product attributes that will satisfy the intended customer. It also refers to specific elements required to produce the product.
2. Objective data and information are irrefutable; if you deny it, exclude it from this process, or believe that you can change/control it, you will be feeding yourself a line of bull. It is what it is.

3. You *can* change your subjective data and information that informed your initial decisions. You can change it because it belongs to you.

4. As an adult, you can literally do whatever you want to do today, this month, this year, and throughout your life. No one needs to empower you; you already have power.

5. Sometimes we hesitate to accept risk because we don't realize how much power we have over our own lives. There are deeply personal decisions to be made. Managing quality requires not only making them, but also accepting 100% responsibility for those decisions.

6. You have the power to choose your every action; however, there are consequences.

7. Your high-level steps represent the steps that occur during the product assembly. This is akin to the assembly line example. Each of those steps should have an intended outcome that moves you and/or your career to the next step.

8. In the manufacturing process guided by the science of quality management, once a manufacturer has designed a process to create a product, they identify potential variations that can influence the process, and therefore, the product.

13

Thinking Is an Ongoing Requirement

"The world as we have created it is a process of our thinking. It cannot be changed without changing our thinking."

—Albert Einstein

There is a part of the chaotic system you exist in that's specifically associated with you. It's a powerful dimension *of sorts* that entered the chaos with you and will move on someday, along with you. It waits to be unleashed as we grow and climb our way up Maslow's hierarchy of needs. Through the years, the concepts of quality management became a highly intuitive part of my day-to-day work. As I applied these concepts during the working hours of my life and led others to do so, I began to realize that I had a system of my own. The concepts crept into my philosophies, mindset, and approach to other areas of my life, including the higher-level aspects of my career, how I viewed my interactions with others, and how I made personal decisions. It became obvious that I could manage my personal quality system to manufacture the authentic life and career that I wanted and needed. Systems can be fantastic and supportive, or they can be terribly flawed. An out-of-control system often feels like no system. It lacks consistency, among other things, and that describes my childhood. Perhaps this is what led me to begin exploring how I could incorporate the framework I was learning about and applying in my professional work on a much more personal level. The illusive *thing* that I had been searching for since childhood had been there all along, hovering just out of reach. It was *my* system, my *own* dimension, something that my mother couldn't mirror for me because the mirror in our family was always facing her. Regardless of your story, there comes a point when the power to define

DOI: 10.4324/9780367855260-13

your own life and career is all yours. Your satisfaction results from a controlled system; an out-of-control system cannot *ensure* anything. Maintaining control of a quality system is an ongoing activity that gets easier over time, especially if you lay the foundation and keep your focus on the crystal ball. It becomes intuitive, like muscle memory. The ability of a company or an individual to create and maintain control of a quality management system boils down to decision making, whether it's during process design or implementation, and regardless of *why* a decision needs to be made, including when faced with an unexpected quality event.

Risk management is a proactive and highly valuable element of a healthy quality system because it supports excellent decision making. Incorporating risk management into your strategy can potentially help avoid special cause variation, and/or ensure that you're well positioned for change when the unexpected hits. In addition to supporting strategic decision making and planning, it works to increase control of your system by decreasing vulnerability to unpleasant surprises you didn't see coming, referred to going forward as career quality events.

Earlier in the book, I shared a career quality event that I experienced: losing my job at Johnson & Johnson due to a corporate-wide downsizing in 2008. Risk management begins with forecasting potential risks to the quality or delivery of your product. A variety of occurrences can put your plans (i.e., process) and career at risk or cause a career quality event, depending on your profession, industry, deliverables, goals, objectives, and more. You may be dealing with a career quality event now; if so, there's no better time to establish a new and improved career development strategy based on the proven science of quality management. *Risk* management is a component of a sound, in-control quality system that focuses on how you can expect the unexpected, by weaving risk into decision making. (As a reminder, you've accepted that common variation will be at play in your process; it's a type of variation you expect and have accounted for. I shared some examples of common variation in Chapter 12.)

WATCH FOR CURVEBALLS

Identifying potential risks can elicit the level of commitment required to fuel change within an organization, and within yourself. Risk assessment and management are consistent with change management principles. Corporations seek to execute planned changes in a systematic way, and to systematically respond to impactful changes that an organization has little or no control over (e.g., legislation, social and political upheaval, the actions of competitors, shifting economic tides and currents, and so on). This is how they manage change. Researchers and practitioners focused on change management typically distinguish between a knee-jerk or reactive response (to a change), and an anticipative or proactive response. As the manufacturer of your 5-star career, a focus on risk identification will enable you to have a more anticipative or proactive response to what is happening around you. Risk management serves to help keep your knees steady during those times when you need to continue moving forward. When deciding to proactively identify risks, it's important to keep a good grip on your crystal ball and continue to consider your intended product as you make decisions.

Exploring potential risk is not *being negative.* It's a proactive approach proven to help *avoid* negative outcomes. Again, I agree that striving to maintain a positive focus and attitude is a great approach. However, you live in a chaotic system that can't possibly be controlled. Believing that you will never feel the sting of a curveball is illogical. Assuming you've decided to go forward with identifying one or more potential risks to your process and 5-star career, it's important to consider two questions for *each* risk:

1. How likely is this to happen based on what you currently know (focus on objective data and information available)?
2. If it occurs, how severely could it impact your process or 5-star career?

Based on these two questions, you will then need to decide if you are willing to accept the risk or not. If you can accept it, you can then consider how you might mitigate the impact if it were to happen. In some ways, this is like establishing a Plan B. If the risk is unacceptable based on the likelihood that it will occur and the severity of its impact, you will need to make a change to your process to avoid *any* possibility of that risk occurring. For example, if part of your plan is to rob a bank, are you willing to accept the risk involved? Sure, robbing a bank may get you the cash needed for law school; however, the associated objective risk is high (e.g., prison, injury, or even death to you or someone else). If I were to add a comment that you *really* shouldn't be robbing banks anyway, that would be my subjective opinion. If *you* believe it's okay to rob a bank (although you may be ignoring some objective data), you can choose to establish that subjective data point for yourself and attempt to rob a bank. As much as I may want to, I can't stop you. If you end up in prison, you're also allowed to change your subjective data (you own it) and decide that robbing a bank was not the best option. In addition to full acceptance or rejection of a risk, you can also choose to mitigate the risk in some way. You'll build in another step or control to specifically address the potential risk. This is different than mitigating impact. Risk mitigation explains why bank robbers have lookouts watching the streets for them. They are trying to minimize risk. To mitigate the impact of the risk in advance, bank robbers may have a lawyer on speed dial.

OUCH! WHO DID THAT?

What is a manufacturer to do when hit with an unpleasant surprise? They manage it. Whether you're starting with a personal system in need of improvement, or you're dealing with a career quality event, there is a process proven to ensure that quality events are addressed in a way that maintains control of a quality system. Risk management is incorporated into this process. In industry, it's referred to as quality event management:

CAREER QUALITY EVENT MANAGEMENT PROCESS

1. Determine the root cause of the issue.
2. Explore and identify practical options/solutions that will address the root cause. These solutions are referred to in quality management as the corrective action. A corrective action corrects the immediate issue.
3. Explore and identify potential preventative action. A preventative action ensures that the issue will not happen again. Some issues may not require preventative action; this is dictated by the root cause.

4. Identify the risks associated with each possible action.
5. Decide to accept, reject, or mitigate the risk associated with each proposed option/solution.
6. Select the corrective, and if applicable, a preventative action. (There can be more than one.)
7. Act.

To determine root cause (step 1), always ask yourself five questions: What? When? Where? Why? And How? It's critical to dissect the career quality event as carefully and accurately as possible, which, in some scenarios, may require that brutal self-reflection you challenged yourself with as you completed the Story Data Mining Tool. Table 13.1 provides examples of how to use these five types of questions to determine root cause. In some cases, answering these questions is easy. In others, it can be extremely challenging.

In industry, once the root cause is clear, actions to address the cause are assigned to a specific individual along with a target date for completion. In your manufacturing shop, all actions are assigned to you. This means that regardless of the root cause, the corrective action must be one that

TABLE 13.1

Useful Questions When Exploring Root Cause

1. **What?**	What is the main topic/focus of the issue? Did I fail to do or produce something or do something incorrectly? What aspect of my personal quality system (i.e., quality policy, process, one of my 5-star career specifications) is most closely related to the main topic of this issue? What am I specifically being asked for or questioned about? Is there any legal or company policy that is not being followed?
2. **When?**	When did or does this occur? Is there any specific timeframe or date associated with this issue? When did this issue first come up?
3. **Where?**	Where is this happening? Is something happening where it shouldn't? Am I in a place I'm not supposed to be for some reason?
4. **Why?**	Why did this happen? Why did those involved make the decision they made in this scenario? If there is a process at play, why is it a process? Why didn't I notice this previously? Why wasn't it addressed sooner? Why do I care? Why might others who are involved care?
5. **How?**	How did this happen? How were decisions made? How did I apply my process and quality policy in this scenario?

you are able to complete. It would be futile to select an action that you can't take. In industry, a company cannot assign responsibility to correct a quality issue that exists within their quality system to someone outside their quality system. They have no authority over the outside entity; it is not part of the quality system that they control. What some people don't realize is that it's all about perspective. For example, let's say that a pharma company requires information from a vendor for the purpose of authoring a report. The FDA requires the pharma company to document their process for generating the report; it is a regulated process. Obtaining the information from the vendor is a major step in that process. Quality management within a regulated industry has the added complexity of documentation. Using a written example to relay how perspective plays a critical role in responsibility is helpful. The *incorrect* way to document this step is as follows, because it places responsibility on an employee and company that is *not* part of the pharma company's quality management system:

Responsible	Action
Vendor company associate, or designee	Provide the required information to the pharma company manager by the tenth business day of each month.

The *correct* way to write this step is as follows, because it places responsibility on the pharma company and their employee, which is within the scope of their quality system:

Responsible	Action
Pharma company manager or designee	Request, via email, all required information from the applicable outside parties by the seventh business day of each month. Include a reminder that the information is due by the tenth business day. If the information is not received by the tenth business day, forward the notification email that was sent to the noncompliant party to the responsible senior manager. Include a note to relay that the issue is being escalated.

Here you see two different perspectives for the same action. The first is passive; it focuses on the *provision* of the information *to* the company. "You're supposed to *provide* it and we're sitting here waiting. If you don't provide it, it's not our fault. It's your responsibility." The second is more active; it states that the company will *obtain* the information.

We are responsible for including the information in our report; therefore, we are going to *obtain* it from you in time to include it. If you don't provide it, we will continue to "obtain" it as best we can. In the end, if you don't provide it, we will get it elsewhere (i.e., we will choose to do business with another vendor) because we are responsible for having it.

If the information is not received on time, the root cause will be that it was not provided by the vendor. The company can request a deeper root cause, but again, if that's not provided, all the company can say is that it wasn't provided. The vendor threw them a curveball; *they* did it. Escalating the issue to the senior manager was a required action. This allows for action to be taken at a higher level, and escalated further, if needed. The most serious action would be the pharma company ending their relationship with the vendor. All of the actions to improve the situation are happening from within the system.

Note: you can escalate issues as well, if needed. For example, you were unjustly let go from your job due to a disability, you can escalate this to your attorney. But just as with the vendor, if for any reason, your attorney is not representing you well, you can impact what is happening by deciding to switch to another attorney.

So, what else can this pharma company do about the report they need to finalize? The vendor is executing work on behalf of the pharma company and there is a contractual agreement; therefore, the pharma company can request that the vendor document a quality event on their end (i.e., in their quality system), and provide a copy. That request is also an action taken by the pharma company. If the vendor continues to be late month after month, the pharma company must continue to act. And guess what? If the pharma company takes action month after month, and it never gets any better, *they* are at fault. This is because the pharma company is responsible for controlling *their* process and their product. If they keep taking the same action every time with no change, it's evident that their system is not working. They are not properly escalating issues, and are not controlling the quality of their process, and potentially of their product. A stronger decision was required, and no one made it.

Note: this is akin to you complaining for years about a situation at work, to no avail. At some point, if you're unhappy, it's your responsibility to make a change; perhaps it's not the best place for you. I stayed in a couple of positions much longer than I should have. I see that now and will not let that happen again. It may be time to go elsewhere. However, don't forget to use objective versus subjective thinking in such a situation. Have the courage to be brutally honest with yourself about the situation and keep your grip on the crystal ball; sometimes leaving is not the best option.

Imagine that the pharma company is required by law to submit the report in question to the FDA by the 20th of every month. If the FDA asks why the reports are consistently late, it is unacceptable for the pharma company to respond by saying that it is the vendor's fault. Submitting the report on time to the FDA is the responsibility of the pharma company according to the law. The pharma company is required to have oversight of the vendor to ensure that the process remains in control and the report is submitted on time. Therefore, if the vendor ultimately cannot provide information on time, the pharma company is responsible for resolving the issue. The only way they can do that, in the face of no improvement, is to find a new vendor. Career quality events must also be viewed from this perspective. In this example, the pharma company's product is on-time FDA submission of a high-quality report. Your end goal is a 5-star career.

For the process above to work as intended when managing a career quality event, you must accept responsibility for all outcomes. You are where the buck stops. This is often the toughest concept to embrace when applying this science personally. I could list a hundred excuses or, as we prefer to call them, reasons, why things go wrong. I could provide a list of career quality events that came at me like curveballs over the last 30 years. I could dissect each one and determine if my approach to managing them followed the process above, and then analyze the information to gain insight on which events derailed me more or longer than others. After you finish reading this book, I encourage you to take the time to do that exercise, if you suspect that it will be a helpful way to further explore your story data and gain insight. I also encourage you to return to your Story Data Mining Tool for the same reason.

IT DOESN'T MATTER *WHO* DID IT

A curveball came out of nowhere! What are *you* going to do now? That's what matters and what should be the focus. "There's nothing I can do," is not an acceptable answer in the context of quality management. Your corrective and preventative actions cannot be assigned to anyone other than yourself; they cannot be assigned to the person, organization, company, etc., who threw the curveball. This trips many people up. Intuitively, it may seem like the person who threw the ball must take responsibility to fix the damage. Well, they could. In many cases, that would be incredibly kind of them. However, you have no authority to make that happen. The only thing you have power over is your actions. Every time you have a career quality event and freeze, you are failing to use your manufacturing power and wasting your banked time. If you let someone else decide what you should do or let them do something for you that is not what you prefer, you are giving away your manufacturing power, throwing your quality system out of control, and wasting your banked time.

Corrective and preventative actions must be based on the options available to *you* within the borders of your personal quality system. Tables 13.2 and 13.3 provide examples of a career quality event managed using two approaches. Table 13.2 includes an event that is *not* managed following the quality event management process described above. Table 13.3 provides an example of how the same career quality event is managed using the quality event management process. As you can imagine, the complexity of this process can vary. I've simplified the examples as much as possible for the purpose of this book.

EVERY ENDING IS A NEW BEGINNING

A 5-star career is worth the time and effort it takes to create and maintain it. Today, the science of quality management weaves through our daily lives, invisible to most people. Millions wake up each day to manage their lives and careers in what seems to be standard ways, approaching both general and career issues that arise using cookie cutter methods. They barrel through despite their approaches not being super exciting or innovative; sometimes it's frustrating. Sometimes it gets downright boring. The masses just get through it, looking forward to the weekend, an upcoming vacation, or anything else they can focus on to add a bit of a thrill to the exercise.

There is always something to work on or towards. I think that speaks to motivation, which we all crave. It's human nature. If you don't see anything ahead, boredom, arrogance, or listlessness can set in. The key is understanding what motivates you and how to keep that motivation going once you've achieved the goals you set ten years ago, five years ago, or last month. As the world around you changes, new scenarios can influence your career. This should not be ignored, even after you've landed in the place your heart once desired.

TABLE 13.2

Management of a Career Quality Event Using an *Intuitive, Unproven* Approach

Event (as privately described to yourself)	I was moved under a new supervisor two months ago. The man is irrational, disorganized, and does not have the experience required to hold the position. Everyone knows that he's one of those charismatic people who can give a speech that sounds fabulous, yet when you really think about, he doesn't really make any solid points. I can't deal with him telling me what to do when I know more than he does. I loved my job and intended to stay here for at least three more years. It was not easy to land this job. I'm not sure what to do. I've never had an experience like this. He is threatening to put me on a performance plan! It's ridiculous. If he fires me or even puts me on that program, my career here or elsewhere could take a serious hit. I felt like I had a 4-star career going, and now I'd have to give it 1 star.
Step 1	**Determine the root cause of the issue. What caused this event?**

He did! He causes me a headache every day. I haven't changed at all. I've always been successful. He showed up and everything went to hell in a handbasket. I've tried to talk to him, but it just doesn't work. He's not abusive or anything like that. I wouldn't say this to anyone, but this guy is a bit of a goofball.

Step 2	**Explore and identify practical options/solutions that will address the root cause. These solutions are referred to in quality management as the corrective action. A corrective action corrects the immediate issue.**

I have no idea what to do. I'm going to complain to my husband every day after work to decompress and get through it. I need to stay at this job. That's my plan. If I must be miserable for a while at least I have my family and coworkers. I can vent. I will just do my best to please the guy, play the game. That's office politics, right? I just need to go to bed earlier. My head hurts all the time. I'll call my doctor tomorrow. Can you hand me that glass of wine?

Step 3	**Explore and identify potential preventative action. A preventative action ensures that the issue will not happen again. Some issues may not require preventative action; this is dictated by the root cause.**

Well, it's bound to happen. Life's a process, right? Next time I need to interview for a job, I'll be careful to watch out for issues like this. The boss makes all the difference in whether you enjoy going to work every day.

Step 4	**Identify the risks associated with each possible action.**

I can't think about the negatives. I need to focus on the positive! I have a respectable job, and a steady salary. I'm still following my plan. I'm lucky, right? I can take dealing with these headaches. It will be worth it one day. Everything happens for a reason.

Step 5	**Decide to accept, reject, or mitigate the risk associated with each proposed option/solution.**

I don't see how this question relates to me. I reject this dude, but I'm stuck with him as my boss. I just have to keep on keeping on and do my best.

Step 6	**Select the corrective and preventative action (if applicable).**

I already told you what I need to do. You're wasting my time with all these questions. Didn't you hear when I said that I have a headache?

Step 7	**Act.**

What do you think I'm doing?

TABLE 13.3

Management of a Career Quality Event *Following* the Science of Quality Management

Career Quality Event Example

Event (as privately described to yourself)	I was moved under a new supervisor two months ago. The man is irrational, disorganized, and does not have the experience required to hold the position. Everyone knows that he's one of those charismatic people who can give a speech that sounds fabulous, yet when you really think about, he didn't really make any solid points. I can't deal with him telling me what to do when I know more than he does. I loved my job and intended to stay here for at least three more years. It was not easy to land this job. I'm not sure what to do. I've never had an experience like this. He is threatening to put me on a performance plan! It's ridiculous. If he fires me or even puts me on that program, my career here or elsewhere could take a serious hit. I felt like I had a 4-star career going, and now I'd have to give it 1 star.
Step 1	**Determine the root cause of the issue. What caused this event?**

What: I suspect the main topic in this issue is that I don't believe he's qualified for his position (subjective).

When: I realized this as soon as I began reporting to him. I have done everything that he has asked me to do. I'm required to do what he asks because he's my superior. I'm also allowed to make decisions according to my own quality policy; however, he's making me uncomfortable by constantly asking me questions. He's my boss yet he's asking me about things he should know.

Where: This usually occurs in his office. He's quieter in meetings, thank goodness.

Why: I think it's happening because he's not qualified for his job (subjective). If I think about it more objectively, maybe he's trying to find out how much I know? Or maybe this is his process for learning the details of a new area of responsibility? I didn't think about it that way because it just makes me uncomfortable. I don't like it. I mentioned it to him a few times, but he didn't seem to pick up my hints that his questions are a bit insulting to me. I care about this because I'm proud of my career and my industry knowledge. I don't like the feeling of being tested all the time. My dad used to do that to me all the time, and I hate it.

How: I assumed that he's not qualified but I haven't seen his resume (objective information). He's related to the company owner (objective). Anyone I've ever known who was related to a leader in the company didn't seem as qualified as the rest of the staff (subjective). When all this started, I forgot to apply a quality management approach. I'm trying to be honest now and make sure I'm assessing this accurately so I can make the best decision.

Step 2	**Explore and identify practical options/solutions that will address the root cause. These solutions are referred to in quality management as the corrective action. A corrective action corrects the immediate issue.**

My options are:

1. Have the courage to be authentic and speak with him about this issue. Tell him why all his questions are difficult for me to process and ask if there might be a way we can work together that would be more efficient.
2. Do the above but begin looking for a new job in case it doesn't work out.
3. Turn in my resignation tomorrow. A huge weight would lift! That would feel so good!

Step 3	**Explore and identify potential preventative action. A preventative action ensures that the issue will not happen again. Some issues may not require preventative action; this is dictated by the root cause.**

- Always apply my quality management approach as soon as I notice an issue.
- If I stay, ensure that I continue to be authentic in my relationship with him.

(Continued)

TABLE 13.3 (CONTINUED)

Management of a Career Quality Event Following the Science of Quality Management

Career Quality Event Example
Step 4   **Identify the risks associated with each possible corrective action.**

1. He could stare at me like a deer in headlights. Nothing could change or he could decide that he doesn't like what I'm saying. Things could get worse.
2. If talking to him doesn't work out, I may not be able to find a comparable job. Also, it could get worse before it gets better (when I find a new job).
3. I could feel so good! However, I would not have a job until I find a new one, which could seriously derail my 5-star career plan.

Step 5   **Decide to accept, reject, or mitigate the risk associated with each proposed option/solution.**

I can accept the risk of option 1 but only with mitigation in place. I can accept the risk associated with option 2. Even if it gets worse, by actively job hunting, I will be in control of my quality system. I will be accepting responsibility to manufacture my 5-star career. No matter how good it would feel tomorrow, I can't accept the risk associated with option 3. I don't know how long it will take to find a new job that supports my process. My quality system would potentially slide out of control, and new risks would be introduced.

Step 6   **Select the corrective and preventative action (if applicable).**

I choose option 2.

Step 7   **Act.**

Tomorrow, I will request a meeting to specifically discuss this with my boss. I will also update my resume and begin my job search process. Wow, I feel so much better. I've regained control of my quality system.

In his book, *Your Erroneous Zones*, Wayne Dyer says that death is the greatest motivator. Most of us don't relish thinking about the end of our lives, but let's do that for a moment. As you move closer to death, the intellectual and emotional package you're carrying will essentially be what you made of your life. Your package doesn't have to be baggage. I want to have a beautiful package that day, one that makes me burst with pride. A day or so before my mother-in-law died, weak as she was in her hospital bed, there was a moment when she lifted both arms into the air, an expression of victory. In a burst of energy, her voice grew stronger and louder as she slowly declared, "I … raised … five … good … people!" Her authentic spirit filled the room with pride and joy that surrounded not only my husband but also me (a woman who wasn't sure that her mother would ever have this thought on her last day). It was one of the most beautiful moments I've ever had the honor to share. I'm determined to feel like my mother-in-law on my last day. The life you hold in your hands that day will be your final product, the result of years of effort, experiences, give and take, decisions, actions, thoughts, and emotions. The work to which you give 8 hours a day, 40 hours a week, or more contributes a substantial portion to the level of satisfaction you will have with that final product. The culmination of a life well lived is the result of a process and a pilgrimage. How better to ensure that your life on any given day, and certainly on your last, meets your 5-star quality expectations than applying the proven science of quality management in a personal way? That's a big goal to tackle, which is why focusing on the quality of your career, an activity that consumes ~50% of the hours you're awake during each work week, is an excellent start.

I've shared pieces of my story throughout this book; you have your own. I hope that you're keeping it close to mind, and that you will continue to do that as you finish this book. There's a time for self-reflection, and making your own choices doesn't make you selfish. There's a brand of self-love we all deserve. For many years, I believed that even the healthy aspects of loving myself were selfish. It's amazing how much our early life can and does inform our future. The good news is that we can continue to learn and grow as individuals. The choice to do so is ours alone. Once childhood is over no one can stop us, nor can anyone do it for us. We either stifle ourselves or give ourselves the gift of growth. I worked at it for many years following my suicide attempt at 19, often feeling that I was walking forward in the dark, bumping into all kinds of things that hurt, facing all kinds of fears, taking risk after risk in the hope that one day it would all make sense. If I was able to develop a valuable personal quality management system, anyone can.

When it comes to my mother, I'm moving closer to the truth. My dad is still with us, happily remarried. He'll be 80 this year. After my parents divorced, he and I grew much closer; it was as if my mother's whirlwind had kept us all at arm's length, despite how much we needed each other. At 19, I began to see who my dad truly was, and how much he loved me. He and I sat next to each other at my brother's funeral in 2012. Just as it was ending, Dad had a heart attack, followed by heart surgery. They told him that the funeral had been a type of stress test. If not for that test, they said he likely would have suffered massive heart failure within months. Although it's a brutally painful reality to consider and verbalize, my dad says, with tears in his eyes, that John saved his life. In the end, I think John saved mine, too.

My mother did not end up with our pastor. In fact, her obsession with him led to a giant split within our church congregation that involved her "going before the elders." After the split, the pastor and his family moved several states away. A year or so ago, it came to my attention that he wrote a book about his ministry. The concepts and activities that he describes align with my memories; yet his story, its tone, the details, and information are nowhere near as terrifying as those my mother described to us every day for years. It turns out that I didn't *have* to be fearful of the demons perched at all corners of my twin bed every night, waiting for me to have one bad thought. The kind our mother said would "open us up" so that they could leap straight into our tiny hearts.

As a young teen, I used to sneak out of our house late at night with a blanket and transistor radio. I'd walk to the nearby elementary school playground, lay on my blanket, listen to the radio, and stare up at the stars, and think. I remember thinking that I was so small lying there, like an ant. Then I imagined that I was a giant leaning against the side of the world. Just for a few minutes, there all alone with no one to think that I might be selfish or arrogant, I gave myself permission to believe that I was *capable* of doing something large for the world someday. I wanted it to be true. I didn't want to be that girl standing in the shadow of a magical woman Jesus loved the most; I wanted to be something of my own. I spent decades researching and analyzing what I know about my mother's story, as well as my own. I looked for answers that would help me to move forward in the ways that I was stuck. Unfortunately, for a long time, I had the wrong customer in mind. Regardless of your story, there comes a turning point, when the power to define your own life and career is *all* yours. The day my brother died was that turning point for me. I knew it was time to somehow pull all the parts of myself together and take my authentic place as the customer of not only my career, but also of the one life I *can* create.

If you recall the woman beneath the green sky, I can tell you that she can clearly see the boat waiting just over her shoulder; I'll be stepping in soon. Knowing what *I* want to say, that *I* can say it, and knowing how *I* want to say it in this book is a large contributor to solidifying my 5-star career. Thank you for being a part of that; you are the reader I've been preparing for my entire life.

KEY POINTS

1. Your satisfaction results from a controlled system; an out-of-control system cannot *ensure* anything. Maintaining control of a quality system is an ongoing activity that gets easier over time, especially

if you lay the foundation and keep your focus on the crystal ball. It becomes intuitive, like muscle memory.

2. The ability of a company or an individual to create and maintain control of a quality management system boils down to decision making, whether it's during process design or implementation, and regardless of *why* a decision needs to be made, including when faced with an unexpected quality event.

3. Risk management serves to help keep your knees steady during those times when you need to continue moving forward.

4. Exploring potential risk is not *being negative*. It's a proactive approach proven to help *avoid* negative outcomes.

5. Whether you're starting with a personal system in need of improvement, or you're dealing with a career quality event, there is a process proven to ensure that quality events are addressed in a way that maintains control of a quality system. Risk management is incorporated into this process. In industry, it's referred to as quality event management.

6. To determine root cause, always ask yourself five questions: What? When? Where? Why? And How?

7. Every time you have a career quality event and freeze, you are failing to use your manufacturing power and wasting your banked time. If you let someone else decide what you should do or let them do something for you that is not what you prefer, you are giving away your manufacturing power, throwing your quality system out of control, and wasting your banked time.

8. Corrective and preventative actions must be based on the options available to *you* within the borders of your personal quality system.

BIBLIOGRAPHY

Wayne W. Dyer. *Your Erroneous Zones: Step-by-Step Advice for Escaping the Trap of Negative Thinking and Taking Control of Your Life* (William Morrow Paperbacks, 2001).

Index

Printed in the United States
by Baker & Taylor Publisher Services